Praise for *Holding Tight, Letting Go*

"Attachment and exploration. Autonomy and relatedness. Connected and apart. Parents, like psychologists, have long recognized the exquisite tension between holding tight and letting go of their children. And they experience this tension becoming rebalanced with each new stage of their child's development. *Holding Tight, Letting Go* is the story of how parents help children become themselves, and Ben Garber unfolds this story with uncommon insight, perspective, and wisdom. He weaves together the discoveries of research, clinical work, and practical experience in an account that is at once informative, engaging, and thought-provoking. Garber profiles the significance of the emotional anchoring that parents provide their children, the importance of providing structure and respecting boundaries, the value of routines and rituals, and what happens when family relationships become disordered. A valuable resource for parents, for those who work with families, and for anybody interested in children's development. Reading it helps all of us take two steps forward (and no steps back)."

— DR. ROSS THOMPSON
Distinguished Professor of Psychology
University of California, Davis

"A poignant voyage into the inner world of parent-child relationships. Drawing on many years of professional experience, Dr. Garber captures with poetic lyricism the human dance of attachment and autonomy, of security and adventure. *Holding Tight, Letting Go* offers a fascinating and crystal clear account of how the rhythms of development play out over the course of a lifetime. Along the way Dr. Garber dispenses solid time-tested advice—from when, why, and how to set limits, to managing bedtime routines and electronic devices—that will help parents shepherd their children to healthy maturity."

— DR. RICHARD A. WARSHAK
author of *Divorce Poison, How to Protect Your Family from Bad-mouthing and Brainwashing,*
Clinical Professor, UT Southwestern Medical Center

"*Holding Tight, Letting Go* is a must read for every parent who recognizes that raising healthy children in the twenty-first century means far more than time-outs and star charts. It offers practical ways for negotiating the difficult choices between protecting their children vs. supporting them as they confront the challenges of modern life. It means protecting our kids from an overwhelming and uncensored flood of media and from very real and immediate physical dangers. This book is the only guide available for the conscientious parent who wants to find a healthy balance between "helicoptering" and abandonment in this age of technology and terror. I highly recommend this book both for professionals, family law attorneys, mediators, and of course parents."

— KIP ZIRKEL, PhD
Wisconsin licensed psychologist
Consultant, The Family and Children's Center
Author, *A Parents' Guide to Custody and Placement"*

"Garber's book *Holding Tight, Letting Go* is so relatable that once you open it, you won't be able to let it go. From one of the first sentences, "It's about knowing when to hold her hand and when not to, when to stand by her side and when to watch from a distance, and when to not watch at all," to the observation that anxiety abounds in our society because with the loss of digital boundaries we are faced with so much information we don't feel safe, I was riveted and reflective."

— **LYNNE KENNEY**, PsyD,
Pediatric Psychologist, co-author, *BLOOM: 50 Things to Say,
Think and Do with Anxious, Angry, and Over-the-Top Kids*

Also by Benjamin D. Garber:

*The Healthy Parent's ABC's:
Healthy Parenting Made Clear and Easy-to-Read*

*Keeping Kids Out of the Middle: Child-Centered
Parenting in the Midst of Conflict, Separation, and Divorce*

*Development Psychology for Family Law Professionals:
Theory, Application, and Best Interests of the Child*

*Ten Child-Centered Forensic Family Evaluation Tools:
An Empirically Annotated User's Guide*

*The Roadmap to the Parenting Plan Worksheet: Putting
Parenting Priorities in the Context of Research, Theory, and Case Law*

HOLDING
TIGHT
—
LETTING
GO

RAISING HEALTHY KIDS
IN ANXIOUS TIMES

Benjamin D. Garber, Ph.D.

UNHOOKED BOOKS
an imprint of High Conflict Institute Press
Scottsdale, Arizona

Library of Congress Control Number: 2015937628

Cover design by Gordan Blazevik
Interior layout by Jeffrey Fuller

Printed in the United States of America

The "me" in me
emerges when we're apart

CONTENTS

INTRODUCTION

I need you when we're apart,
but need to be apart
when we're together.

Psychology is the science of separation.

The study of human development and relationships is ultimately the study of how we grow a "self," unique from those around us. It took me almost sixty years living as a human being, forty of those working as a psychologist, to realize this essential fact. But I'm not alone. As a species, we humans know more about Alpha Centauri, long extinct dinosaurs, and subatomic particles than we do about "self" for one very good reason: It's much easier to look in a microscope or a telescope than it is to look in a mirror.

"Self," as I use it throughout this book, is the subjective and elusive experience of completeness that most humans seek. It is the identity we fear is so vulnerable in this digital age. It is who I am different from you and him and her and the furniture.

Self is to the body like the rider is to the racehorse: Under the best of circumstances, self gradually learns how to control impulses and to regulate needs and manage the physical world before the inescapable changes associated with age unseat the rider.

Self emerges reflexively as a result of its own awareness. The process is marked by a million back-and-forth events. Separations and reunions. We recognize a handful of these as milestones celebrated with cake and ice cream, balloons and gifts. Birthdays and graduations. The first day of kindergarten. Marriage. Retirement. Death. The vast majority of these events, however, slip by beneath the radar. These are the everyday, two-steps-forward, one-step-back, trial-and-error lunges toward separateness. Trying a new food. Joining a team. Making a friend. Having an argument. Losing a friend. I believe that every one of these, from birth through death, across history and cultures, shares a single universal dynamic: the push-pull ambivalence of holding tight and letting go.

Holding tight and letting go.

I've made a career writing and speaking and consulting with families and institutions about raising healthy children. As my own self has emerged, I've come to think of parenting and co-parenting less in terms of time-outs, reward charts, and bedtime rituals, and more as the essential process of holding tight and letting go. Thus, I think of this book as the guidelines for those of us with the awesome responsibility of helping another human being grow his or her own self.

On Ages and Stages

Don't be confused: Psychology textbooks and college courses in human development commonly and correctly distinguish stages of growing up, the same way that an elevator rises from one floor to the next. Thinking grows from concrete to abstract. Morality grows from trust to integrity. Even physical development is discussed as if infancy and adolescence were as distinct as the caterpillar is from the butterfly.

While it's certainly easier to think of growing up as occurring in a sequential, stepwise manner, this concept is somewhat misleading. No one goes to sleep one night in the sensorimotor stage of cognitive development and wakes up the next morning in the preoperational stage. Development is a much more gradual two-steps-forward, one-step-back process of change that occurs in the context of relationships.

Our experience of social connections can help or hinder development. When we feel safe and secure, we become free to explore new ways of thinking and behaving; to take the elevator to a new floor for at least a brief visit. By contrast, when our relationships are insecure—when the world seems scary, threatening, and uncertain—we retreat and resist change and growth and development.

This book is not about discrete stages or ages. It is about the single powerful and pervasive dynamic that underlies the process of growing up from conception through the senior years and death. It's about the necessary and natural tension between feeling held tight and being let go.

When and how we decide to hold our children tight or to let them go must certainly vary as our own needs change, as our children's abilities emerge, and as the world around us allows, but the process is timeless, universal, and unchanging. It was no different when ancient humans decided whether their children were ready to leave the cave and it will be no different when our grandchildren's grandchildren decide whether their children are ready to explore new virtual worlds. Here and now today, even as you read this book, it is the tension that connects you and your child, whether she is asleep in your lap or off with her own children half a world away.

A Word about Words

This book is full of hypothetical vignettes intended to illustrate the yo-yo, back-and-forth process that is holding tight, letting go. I often refer generically to Billy and Bobby or Mom and Dad, or Honey and Sally. Now and again I mention Grandma or Grandpa as well. Please don't focus on the gender or generation or the names. Aside from the physiology specific to gestation and birth, nothing in this volume should be construed as specific to caregivers of either sex or any generation. "Billy" and "Sally" and a handful of other names I use are characters I dreamed up for the purpose of illustration only.

By the same token, except when discussing marriage and divorce specifically, the legal status of the relationship between adults who care for a given child is unimportant. Marriage is an artificial construct created by society, instituted by the government, and enforced by the courts that has no necessary meaning to our children. Billy and Sally don't care whether Mom and Dad are never-married, presently married, or divorced. What they care about and what they need is a modicum of cooperation, communication, and consistency between their caregivers so that they can feel held tight.

More generally, I take full responsibility for the words you'll read here, although not the concepts. This book is an amalgam of ideas that should be credited to a hundred experts and theoreticians and clinicians and a thousand parents who have so generously allowed me into their lives. I would like to credit them all, but space and confidentiality make this impossible.

I must, however, credit three very distinct women.

The first is a pioneer developmental ethologist and the mother of attachment theory, Mary Ainsworth. Although we never met, I consider Dr. Ainsworth's successes teaching the world about parent-child bonds as influential in psychology as Einstein's work is in physics or Mozart's work is in music. Although I choose different metaphors, most of what I get right here should be credited to Ainsworth and colleagues. Any parts that I get wrong are entirely my own fault.

The second woman to be credited is the dynamo who made this volume happen. Megan Hunter of Unhooked Books is an amazing entrepreneur, editor, publisher, publicist, cheerleader, bookseller, and friend all rolled into one. If not for Megan's interminable optimism, enthusiasm, and support, your hands would now be empty.

The third and most important woman I am indebted to is my wife, Laura. She is the emotional anchor any person would long for and far greater than I deserve. She has let me go over and over again to explore my ideas and ambitions, and every single time she is there to hold me tight when I fall down. Although Ainsworth must be credited with the theory and Hunter must be credited with the production, Laura must be credited with giving me the confidence to go on this long explore.

I wish you, dear reader, a Laura of your own.

About the metaphors and squibs that punctuate this volume: Our society commonly makes an artificial distinction between feeling and thinking, disparaging affect and over-investing in analysis. In truth, emotion is our first language and the foundation upon which cognition is built. Identity emerges in the tension between the two, pulled one way by instinct and the other by intellect. Thus, neither the academics nor the poets can ever adequately answer the question "who am I?" without the other. A real understanding of self calls for an amalgam of the emotionally evocative and the scientifically sound.

This book strives to be just such an alloy of fact and feeling. I freely mix research and theory with metaphor and story-telling in an unabashed effort to speak both to your brain and to your gut. I open and close the book and each chapter with an observation or an insight—a squib (in my words) intended to set the stage for the ideas that follow. It is my sincere hope that by weaving data and dreams together, I might better communicate to the whole of you.

BDG
September, 2015

· · · · · · · · · ·

CHAPTER ONE

TAKING OFF
THE TRAINING WHEELS

Growing up is a poorly choreographed dance:
When you hold her tight, she demands to be let go.
When you let her go, she cries to be held tight.

This book is about your child's first steps.

It's about putting her on the school bus on her first day of kindergarten, and dropping her off at summer camp. It's about telling her "no," she can't drive to her friend's house, and it's about walking her down the aisle.

It's about which video games she can play and which movies she can watch and which friends she can hang out with. It's about urging her to try out for the play and the soccer team, moving her into her dorm room, and being there to comfort her when she's scared and sick and lonely.

It's about knowing when to hold her hand and when not to, when to stand by her side and when to watch from a distance, and when to not watch at all.

This book is *not* about everything human; it's about that single, powerful dynamic upon which everything human is built. It's about the push-pull, back-and-forth ambivalence that characterizes every relationship and is most obvious as it occurs between parent and child. It's about holding tight and letting go.

Listen: It's a warm Saturday morning in late spring. There's a lawn mower buzzing away in the distance. Fluffy white clouds dot a perfect blue sky.

The training wheels have finally come off. Your little girl is wearing her pink princess helmet and a look that conveys both determination and terror. You jog alongside the bicycle, one hand clenched over the handlebars, the other holding the pink plastic seat, offering advice and encouragement. Smiling, even though we all know how this story goes.

"You can do it! Pedal harder!"

You've always been there to protect her, to bandage the boo-boos. You'd throw yourself in front on an oncoming car to save her. So why, now, are you launching her toward certain harm? She's going to fall. Probably skin a knee. Maybe bruise an elbow.

Every scratch and scrape she's ever had flashes through your mind. Twice you rushed her to the ER. You'll never forget her look of shock and betrayal when she broke her ankle. The screams and tears were bad enough, but that look said, "How could you let this happen to me? I thought you were here to keep me safe!" That was the hardest to swallow.

You're starting to breathe hard now. Is it the exertion or anxiety? Part of you wants to stop, to find the wrench and put the training wheels back on. She's safe that way. Well, *safer* at least. But another part of you understands how much she wants this new freedom. She wants to ride a big girl bike just like all the other kids in the neighborhood.

"I'm doing it, Mommy!" You recognize her squeaky, high tone. She's scared but she wants this so much.

"You're doing great, sweetie!"

Catastrophes run through your brain: Are the tires inflated? Are her brakes working? Does she remember how to use them? What if she hits her head? What if a car veers onto the sidewalk? What if she steers into the street? I should have brought my cell phone to call 9-1-1. If she hurts her back, should I move her or keep her still? I wonder if these neighbors are home if I need a phone.

But you urge her on anyway: "That's it! Pedal harder!"

Somewhere deep inside, you know that this is about growing up. Today it's a two-wheeler. Tomorrow she'll get her license. Then she'll be off to college or a job. Maybe she'll get married. Will she have kids of her own? I hope she's better at teaching them to ride. More confident. Less panicky.

"Look, Mommy! I'm doing it!"

You must let go.

Your mom did. You remember her running alongside your bike. It was autumn. Crunchy leaves underfoot. You were scared and excited but she was right there, by your side, and then suddenly she wasn't and you were thrilled—flying like the wind for a moment that lasted forever until it stopped. Knee on pavement. Pedal against shin. Your favorite jeans torn. You knew that she would let go. You even told her to let go, but you were shocked when she did, that she let you fall. But then she was there once more. Holding you and comforting you and crying herself. And then you were back on the seat somehow and trying again.

"Let go, Mommy!"

No. Hold her tight. Keep her safe. She's going to fall.

Maybe I should have an ambulance standing by, just in case. Is her shoelace coming undone? It'll get caught in the pedals. She'll be thrown into traffic. And there's a bus coming toward us! It's so big and she's so small. We should stop. Tie her shoe. Check the brakes. Wait for the bus to pass. Wait for her to get bigger. We can try again tomorrow. Or next year.

"Let me go, Mommy! I'm doing it!"

Fear and excitement push-pull in your head. Hold her tight. Let her go.

And then she's off. Out of your hands. Screaming her excitement and terror and freedom and pride. She sticks her tongue out between pursed lips in concentration, just like her dad does. Her little fists are white with pressure on the handlebars, wind whipping her hair out behind her. You can see through your own tears that she is doing it. She's on her own.

She glances back to make sure that you're looking and in that moment you remember doing the same thing a million years ago. Your mom was there, wiping her hands on her jeans, cheering and clapping for you, watching you go. Then it happens and you are powerless to do anything but watch. The handlebars turn. The front wheel shifts. She hits a divot in the pavement, and the bike collapses sideways on top of her, her body falling in a blur of pink and fear. Her screams blame you. How could you let her go? How could you betray her like this? Her cries are shrill, cutting to your core.

Oh my god—she's hurt!

There's blood on both knees and tears in her eyes, but she's conscious. Her arms and legs are still attached and bend where they're supposed to. And she's both smiling and crying. Her cheeks are bright red with embarrassment or accomplishment or windburn or all three. She clings to your neck like she did on the first day of preschool, like she did when you left her with her first babysitter. Her hair tickles your cheek and she's talking through her tears.

"Did you see? I did it, Mommy!"

Deep breath. She's okay.

Reassuring words. A kiss on the nose and you gently peel her off and settle her on the grass. Straighten her helmet. The knee is fine. Maybe that's paint from the craft closet, not blood. Her hand is scraped red but you kiss it better and remind her of the success. "You did it, kiddo! You were riding all by yourself!"

Then the hard part: "Ready to try again?"

She's ready. You're scared. But you smile and joke and put her back on the pink plastic seat. Straighten yourself up. Deep breath. Jog alongside again, holding tight until you have to let go.

Holding Tight, Letting Go is about taking off the training wheels. It's about the necessary and natural tension that defines growing up and growing apart. It's about the constantly shifting pressure between separation and reunion. Being together and being apart. "Me" versus "us." It's about the back-and-forth two-step that describes every parent-child relationship everywhere through all of time. Whether it's the baby's first steps or the teenager's first date, or the simple, repetitive, and frustrating process of getting her off to school in the morning, the dance is the same.

You push her away but she clings and cries.

She pulls away but you demand that she stay.

Somehow, through all the fear and excitement, tears and yelling, terror and pride, the ambivalence resolves. The milestone is achieved. The training wheels come off. The sleepover is managed. The first day passes. The milestone is accomplished and then on to the next. Two steps forward, one step back in the best of times and gradually, back and forth, parent and child master another degree of freedom.

Along the way, roles change. Rules are modified. Relationships are redefined. This book is about that too. It's not only about how children grow up, but also about how families grow up. How identity shapes personality and both adapt in the context of relationships. It's not only about how parents shape who their children become, but how our children shape who we are as well.

This dance of ambivalence is the essential drama of humanity, replayed over and over again from that first cry of birth through our last breath. It's the tug-of-war that echoes through all of our lives and all of our relationships. It's how identity emerges, self-esteem is built, and confidence is fueled. It's how we, as parents, manage and communicate our anxiety to our kids in healthy ways so that they can do the same someday with theirs.

In the end, this book is not about learning to ride a bike as much as it is about how and when we let the bike-rider go, even though we know she's going to tumble and cry and look for reassurance. It's about finding a safe and healthy balance between holding tight and letting go, crossing your fingers and holding your breath and saying a prayer that she'll be okay. It's about trusting that all the lessons you've taught her will be enough because the world that she's inheriting is at least as full of beauty as it is of danger.

Real and Imagined Dangers

Two motives drive us to hold our children tight. The first is selfish and primitive and destructive.

No one likes to share their toys. We teach toddlers to take turns, to wait in line, and to share because that's how living together works. At age three, it's easy to mistake the blue shovel in the sandbox or the baby doll with the blond hair as "mineminemine," which, as any preschool teacher will testify, is certainly sufficient reason to kick all who dare come close.

By middle school, most of us are fairly well socialized. We learn that if we want to fit in, we need to let the other kids have a turn. We practice sharing and gift giving and begin to understand loss. A favorite gadget is misplaced. A treasured belonging is stolen. A pet dies. A best friend moves far away. Each of these moments is a tragedy marked by tears or rage or grief. A parent's job is sometimes to patch the wound, but more often simply to help the child manage the pain. To cope with letting go.

But then high school and hormones complicate the process. After ten or twelve or fourteen years of practice, most kids are pretty good at letting go. Sharing and taking turns. Until biology interrupts with its visible, audible, and even olfactory evidence of puberty. Breasts and zits and cracking voices and body odor reignite the primitive need for exclusive ownership, only now it's not about the blue shovel. It's about finding a partner.

Dating is about marking your territory, however briefly. It's about posting a "no trespassing" sign on another human being. Dating is about *not* sharing until one partner lets the other go.

Dating, like taking the training wheels off the bike, inevitably leads to getting hurt. Rejection, humiliation, and long, swooning days of poor-me spent in candlelit rooms listening to self-indulgent music can be so much more difficult than skinned knees and scraped palms.

Just like learning to ride a two-wheeler, dating is practice. Holding tight and letting go. Until you hold tight and swear to never let go.

Marriage is the real deal. It's a legally sanctioned, church-endorsed, publicly witnessed promise *not* to share. Long ago, marriage was a form of ownership. The man owned the wife and the children just like cows and horses. Conscience and culture have since made matrimony into something a bit more equitable, but no less exclusive.

Enter Bouncing Baby Billy, stage left.

The hormones associated with pregnancy and childbirth (for men and women both) induce nesting. A biological drive to build the protective walls around family high and strong. To accumulate stuff the way a bear eats in advance of a long winter's hibernation. Once upon a time that may have meant curing meat and salting fish and stacking firewood in anticipation of months devoted to a helpless child. Today it means spending recklessly on tiny, frilly, hypoallergenic outfits and wireless HD cloud-based monitors and lots of brightly colored, expert-endorsed plastic manipulables. One way or another, the message is the same: mineminemine.

The new baby belongs to Mom and Dad (or Mom and Mom, or Dad and Dad, or either one alone without a partner) the same way the blue shovel belonged to the four-year-old. Both are precious. Neither is actually owned.

Except sometimes.

Sometimes, some parents can't let go. These parents mistake the child as a thing to be owned. Mom (or Dad) holds Bouncing Baby Billy and won't let go. The roles are reversed. She needs him for her sense of well-being. As Billy grows, Mom's clinginess becomes first over-protectiveness and then pathological. She doesn't send Billy to preschool. Okay. Plenty of children don't go to preschool. Then she won't let him go to kindergarten. Or on playdates. She insists on homeschooling not because she finds the local schools lacking, not due to a religious conviction, not because he has a terrible illness, but because she needs him close by for her sake. She can't let go.

Billy is taught that he is Mommy's helper—her friend or partner or nurse. That leaving her could mean losing her. If he were away, she might drink or drug or die. For this child, the training wheels never come off. At conception he was physically a part of his mother and by age five or, left unchecked, long into adulthood, he is still just as completely a part of her.

This is the first of two motives that drives some parents to hold their children tight. An adult's primitive and unhealthy need to feel needed thrust upon a child. A selfish drive that enlists a son or daughter to serve the parent's needs, where a healthy parent's job is to serve the child's needs.

The second motive that can inhibit letting go is likely more familiar and far more common. In fact, it may be a universal experience among parents throughout time.

Terror

For most of us, letting go is hard not because we need our children to make us feel whole, but because we can't stand the idea that they could get hurt.

We know that our children are weak and vulnerable and born into a very scary world. That was as true for the caveman who needed to protect his young from wolves and lions as it is for you I today. The predators of the past may no longer pose a real threat, but that doesn't mean the world is any safer. If anything, the dangers that our children face are more varied and far less obvious.

The caveman could hear the howl of a hungry wolf pack. He could see, hear, and smell a menacing predator. He could run and hide or fight these threats off, so it was easy to know when to let go. But lead poisoning happens without warning. Internet pornography appears without howled alarms. Radon and carbon monoxide kill silently.

The pedophile on the playground looks like any other well-intended grown-up until he doesn't. His approach is innocuous and benign, camouflaged among caregivers better than any wolf in the woods.

The ride to school on that big yellow bus is laughing and familiar and convenient until the crash and then you wonder why it had no seat belts. Why you didn't drive your son to school yourself? Why you didn't keep him home and safe in the first place?

Anxiety in the form of fear motivates us to hold our children tight. Terror motivates us to resist letting them go. You can leave the training wheels on forever and she'll be far less likely to fall and skin her knee. You could forbid her from riding a bike at all or from leaving the house or even from leaving your side. You could lock her in a sterile bubble far from most dangers but, in so doing, you become a danger yourself.

Holding on too long can be as harmful as letting go too soon.

Is it cautious or crazy to use a video monitor in the baby's room? To track your grade schooler's cell phone by GPS? To review your teenager's URLs and tweets and texts? Is it protective or pathological to insist on meeting the parents before the sleepover? To demand that your son call you once a day from summer camp? That your daughter Skype with you twice a week from college? To move in to the house next door when she's married and living with her husband?

For both you and the caveman, and for every parent in between and yet to come, letting go is in part about evaluating the threat and in part about managing anxiety. It's a balancing act with no certain rights or wrongs within obvious extremes.

Practical Pointer:
BEING PREPARED BUT NOT ANXIOUS

There have always been and always will be threats in the world around us. Some threats are as unlikely as being struck by lightning; others are as common as car accidents. In order to let your children go even briefly, you'll need them to be well prepared but not nervous. You're much more likely to accomplish this goal if safety and preparedness are routine and matter-of-fact parts of your daily life.

Don't argue about bike helmets, seat belts and car seats, floatation devices and sunscreen. These and similar precautions must be as obvious and necessary as wearing pants. No helmet? No riding. Period. No seat belt? The car doesn't move. Period. There's no negotiating. There are no exceptions. There's no argument. As with any limit, your kids will test you on the need for these protections. If it's about safety, you must follow through every single time.

Your emotions and behavior are key. Not only does this mean that you have to practice what you preach—yes, that means you do wear your seat belt 100 percent of the time—you have to do so without emotion. Your anxiety is contagious. If snapping on a seat belt or crossing the street or driving a car or being near water or in crowds makes you anxious, expect that your kids will become anxious doing these things as well.

Anxiety is to conflict like gasoline is to fire. If you're nervous, your kids will be nervous and there will be an argument.

. . . .

CHAPTER TWO

DRIP, DRIP

As infants, we are everything.
We are all-powerful and all-knowing, kings of the universe.
Maturity is the relief of learning that this isn't so.

The constant, back-and-forth tension between holding tight and letting go serves a purpose. Two steps forward, one step back. Healthy
human development is an excited and terrified, brave and embarrassed, determined and disgraced jerky forward movement toward
autonomy: Selfness. A gut-level confidence about who I am and how
I fit in to the world that I inhabit.

We are each launched forward into development, halting and
uncertain, out of an "oceanic" sense of self. The term is credited to
Sigmund Freud, the father of contemporary psychotherapy. Listening
to his patients' accounts of their earliest memories, Freud intuited that
the pre-verbal child's experience is global and undifferentiated. He
suggested that our earliest awareness is all-encompassing, utterly me-
centered, and lacking all distinction between self and not-self.

Oceanic.

It makes sense. For weeks or months prior to birth, the fetus's
experience is oceanic—floating in an undifferentiated, seemingly
timeless universe. There is no not-me. Hunger and satiation, pain and
release, fatigue and rest are seamlessly connected. Mother and child

are literally inseparable; physically and psychologically ONE. In this universe there can be neither holding tight nor letting go. That tension requires at least two participants. For an infinite moment, there is only ONE.

Ask any newborn and the answer you'll hear is, "I am everything and everything is me." (Of course, he'll imagine that the question was his own.)

Our culture has long been embroiled in an impossible debate about if and when the not-yet-born human is biologically, legally, or morally a person. Politics and religion and the courts may someday settle the matter, but psychology has known the answer for decades: There can be no "self" before that first and most traumatic experience of letting go.

Or even long thereafter.

Birth is less the landmark emergence of self than it is the shocking separation of need from need fulfillment. It results in an incomprehensible and intolerable and completely unfamiliar interruption of comfort. For the first time, hunger goes unfulfilled. Exhaustion occurs without rest. Pain strikes without relief. Need is separated from immediate satisfaction.

Before birth, there is simply no reason to signal need. After birth, an infant who fails to signal her needs will die. Thus, we have evolved in such a way that infants now express their needs, creating two contemporary realities. Number one: Children are noisy. No matter how much sleep you lose, no matter how often you're interrupted, this is good. Crying and whining and cooing are the cornerstones of communication. More than just language, communication is about relationships. Crying does more than express need; it asks for a response. Infants learn through repetition that crying brings food (or other relief), which, in turn, is associated with a particular person's scent, touch, and appearance. Very soon, those same sensory cues bring pleasure even in the absence of need. This is the foundation of the child's first attachment relationship.

Number two: The delay that occurs between need expression and need fulfillment begins to teach babies to delay gratification. Back in the good old days, the womb provided instant relief. Now need goes unfulfilled, at least for a time, which prompts screams and tears. This, in turn, prompts you as the parent to look for the remote, push pause, put down your cell phone, stand and cross the room to get a bottle, calling out soothing, melodic reassurances all the while.

"It's okay, sweet nookums. Mommy's coming. Who's the most handsome boy on the planet? You are, of course!"

Sweet nookums associates that voice and that tone with food. Diminished discomfort. Satiation. Pleasure. Soon enough that voice will help to calm him, at least briefly, by association—even in the absence of food.

Hunger. Cry. Delay. Satiation.

Pain. Cry. Delay. Relief.

Need and need fulfillment are separate.

Could it be that me and not-me are separate?

Not-me appears, then disappears. Appears, then disappears. This is where and when and how it all begins. Holding tight. Letting go.

Self emerges gradually out of this tension, in fits and starts, as a by-product of the back-and-forth, push-pull recurring tension between holding tight and letting go. Holding tight and letting go. Over and over and over again. As many times and in as many different ways as this drama is played out through the lifespan, it is never as powerful and complete and irreversible as when it first occurs in the terrible insult that is birth.

Do this: Get a cup of water. Dip the tip of a finger in the liquid; then pull it out slowly and smoothly. The drip clinging to the end of your finger has an identity. Maybe not a name or a social security number or a Twitter handle, but a bounded separateness from the world in which it exists. If your vision is good enough, you can see the edges where the drip stops and your finger begins. The drip is discrete, separate, and autonomous.

Now gently wiggle the finger so that the drip falls back into the cup.

You won't see it, but there is a fleeting moment when the intact drip collides with the surface of the liquid below. If it were a coin or a ball or a rock, there would be a splash, but the object would maintain its identity. You could find it and retrieve it whole and intact. In or out of the water, the object would remain bounded and distinct.

Not the drip. The drip is immediately and seamlessly consumed. Its identity is lost. If you'd dropped a grain of sand back onto the beach, that particular grain might be indistinguishable and irretrievable, but its integrity would go unchanged. It does exist separate and whole somewhere amidst the crowd of other grains that make up the beach. The drip does not.

The drip hits the water and loses its identity. It becomes unbounded. If I asked you to find the same drip again, you'd reasonably raise a puzzled eyebrow and admit that the task is impossible. That unique drip no longer exists.

This is all of child development in reverse.

The infant exists in that infinite, oceanic, and unbounded state like the yet-to-be drip in the cup of water until it is wrenched away at the moment of birth. The body demands separateness, but the self is unprepared. Gone suddenly is the perfectly climate-controlled, scuba-like, weightless comfort, complete with 24/7 maid service. Gone suddenly are the muffled sounds and muted lights. The newborn is abruptly thrust into a world that startles, threatens, and moves. The warm bath that insulated and cushioned and nurtured is replaced by temperature and textures that scrape and chafe and burn. Where taste and smell were constant and indistinct, odors now assault and excite and repulse. Where sounds were muted, now they're harsh. Some are familiar and soothing, but most clamor and clash. Where there was gentle weightlessness, floating in a bath, now there is motion and direction; jerky starts and stops.

All of these and more overwhelming neonatal sensory experiences mean separateness. Drip-ness. For the child, birth is the experience of being physically torn apart. An inalterable loss of an incomparable security. It is being thrust away from all that is familiar, safe, and tolerable and set adrift, left to cling in some shallow way to the lost part of self that will eventually be called Mom and, years later, might fully be accepted as a person separate and apart.

But our little science experiment with the cup of water fails in at least one important way. You lifted the drip away from the water in a single, smooth motion—as if the development from birth to autonomous self occurred in a moment. While these are the two endpoints of the process of growing up, the reality is quite different. In truth, the seventy or eighty or ninety years in between are marked by a million forward-and-back, forward-and-back jerks toward separation.

Hold me tight.

Let me go.

Hold me tight.

Let me go.

Practical Pointer:

WE ALL MUST RETURN TO THE OCEAN NOW AND THEN

We fight for greater and greater independence, even as we yearn to be held tight and cared for. This is the essential tension that underlies all of human development and relationships. We want to emerge from the ocean as a drip, whole and separate, but we relish those moments when we are once again immersed.

Everyone needs the relief and comfort of returning to that oceanic state now and again. Some psychologists argue that sleep is just such a surrender of self and a return to an oceanic state. More concretely, we all need a vacation from time to time. A release from the demands of maturity. A chance to let our hair down (at least those of us who still have some), to take a deep breath, hold it, and let it out oh-so-slowly. You and I get this when we take a walk or go out for the evening or away for a weekend or a week. For some, it's a massage or a concert or a good book. For others it's two weeks in Europe. Not surprisingly, many people find that being in or on or near water—especially the ocean—brings with it that deep-breath, whole-body relief.

And our kids? Just because a day at school or a playdate with a neighbor seems like nothing compared to your workday, don't assume that these activities provide your son or daughter with

21

that same sort of relief and release. These activities probably demand their mature best.

Children usually find release when they know that their caregivers are in charge—when they know that the world is secure. They may not admit it and they often will resist it, but cuddling at bedtime or on the couch while watching a movie can be as critical to their emotional well-being as fruit and vegetables and exercise are to their physical well-being.

. . . .

CHAPTER THREE

ON BECOMING AN ANCHOR

There can be no distance or destination
until you have a home.

A healthy parent is an emotional anchor. Solid and reliable. Firm and constant. Stable and secure.

An anchor keeps a boat in place. Connected by a rope, the boat is allowed to drift only so far in any direction around its center. You, the parent, are that emotional center. You are your sons' and daughters' secure base. They may not say it and they will fight against it, but your ability to anchor your children emotionally today will allow them to feel secure and confident tomorrow.

The rope that connects you to your kids is always present. It began as an umbilical cord—an actual, physical channel communicating nurturance from mother to child. Birth is every child's first terrifying and miraculous experience of letting go. A physical connection is replaced by something invisible and intangible and often delayed, but no less nurturing. That invisible connection—the emotional umbilicus that connects each of us to our psychological anchors—grows and changes but persists through childhood and adulthood and even after death.

Don't ask your kids. Little ones won't understand the idea of an "emotional anchor." Older kids might grasp the metaphor but be embarrassed by its implications. Look instead within and ask yourself:

Who are my emotional anchors?

The answer becomes evident in times of stress.

When life is good—when your belly is full and you're rested and in good health; when the environment is familiar and safe; when relationships are calm and reliable—we feel free to explore and learn and grow. We test our limits; we try out new ways of thinking and behaving. When life is good, we allow ourselves to float out to the full extent of the anchor rope and then some. We test limits.

But when stress hits—when we experience hunger, exhaustion, illness, or pain; when the world is unfamiliar and relationships feel fragile or threatening—we retreat closer to our anchors. When stress hits, we invest our finite energies in safety, and at these times we are less likely to explore and grow and learn. Our bodies react reflexively, sending blood away from our brains to fuel the muscles that allow us to fight or flee. We seek out that which is familiar and comforting, safe and reassuring.

Watch any fifteen- to eighteen-month-old in his mother's arms as he encounters an unfamiliar place. He may seem clingy at first, clutching his anchor for safety and support. With time, he'll first explore the setting visually, studying faces and orienting to sounds. If all is well, he'll begin to fuss, asking to be let down.

If Mom puts the toddler down—let's call him Bouncing Baby Billy—he'll begin to explore. One step away, then three, then ten. Some kids will be bolder, more audacious. Others, more cautious. Either way, at some point every healthy child will check back visually with Mom as they go.

Is she still there? Am I safe?

Then anxiety hits. Stress. A sudden movement. A tumble. Fatigue. Hunger. Baby Billy will scramble back to Mom or land on his bottom crying to be retrieved, learning to associate tears with pick-up. Or perhaps Mom is the one who becomes anxious. A stranger enters the room. The child approaches something dangerous. Mom calls the baby back or scoops him up, soothing and holding him tight. Either way, mother and child are reunited. The baby is anchored again. Reassured even if he is screaming to be let go.

Holding tight. Letting go.

If we could look down from above and make a time-lapse video of parent and child spanning years, we'd see concentric circles. The setting would change from kitchen to bedroom to living room. From carpool line to classroom to church. From scout troop to soccer practice to dance recital. The child would grow and the parent would age. The clothes, the seasons, and the years would all change, but the essential geometry would remain the same: Child moves away from parent and then returns to center. Away and back. Away and back. Further and further each time.

The story is the same in infancy as the baby crawls away, looks around, and then returns to center. In grade school, the child discovers peers' birthday parties and playdates, class field trips and sleepovers. In high school, he discovers and explores summer camp, class trips, and dating; groups, clubs, and gangs. And driving. The radius of those concentric circles centered around the anchor increases by magnitudes when he finally possesses that coveted license.

In young adulthood, the child moves even further afield toward college and work, dormitories and apartments, best friends and girlfriends. Spring break in Florida. A semester abroad in Europe. Through it all, the anchor rope remains intact. Someday, perhaps, our kids will visit other planets but even then, measuring the radius of their movement in light years, the story will be the same.

Committed adult relationships (with or without marriage) complicate the story. Establishing whether your spouse replaces, or complements, or remains secondary to your childhood anchors causes a great deal of adult conflict. The answer is probably specific to each family and determined in part by culture, but the process remains unchanged. Even as adults, we move away from our anchors and then back, over and over again.

Holding tight and letting go.

And then our kids have kids of their own and become those children's anchors. This has gone on, generation after generation, for the history of the species. Parents anchoring children who become parents who anchor their children, like so many dominoes in a line.

Add stress and each domino falls back, resting on the one before. Child on parent.

How do I know?

I know because, like you, when I look in the mirror I see my own see mom or dad looking back. When I have a success, a very quiet voice in the very back of my brain wonders what my mom or dad would think. When I'm stressed, like you, I catch myself wanting a parent to take care of me. And, most tangibly, I know because of the things that I wear and the things that I carry.

Practical Pointer:

ARE WE TOO ANCHORED?

The balance between holding tight and letting go means that we must help our children feel anchored, but we must also help them to feel safe being apart. In today's world of Wi-Fi connections, FaceTiming and Skyping, and text messaging, holding tight has become easier and easier. Chapter 9 talks about some creative ways to help children feel more connected.

But how can we help children disconnect and still feel safe? How can you peel that cling-on toddler off your leg or kick the house-bound teenager out of his room?

The answer has three essential parts:

1. Set the limit calmly, clearly, consistently, and firmly. "I need some time alone in the bathroom," or "I'm turning off my phone except for real emergencies until five-zero-zero on the micro-wave clock," or "Today is a no-texting day."

2. Make reconnecting predictable and the time apart manageable. A younger and less emotionally mature child may only be able to manage five minutes apart today. An older and more emotionally mature child might manage an hour or an afternoon or a day. In either case, be clear about when and where you'll next be available.

3. Tolerate the rage and grief. Letting a child go who wants to be held tight can ignite very powerful emotions. Be confident and

clear. Offer support but don't cave. Reassure that he'll be fine; then follow through.

Making this work can be especially important when parents live apart and a child resists leaving one parent to spend time with the other. It's easy to mistake the child's separation anxiety for evidence that the other parent is somehow hurtful. Be clear: "You're going with your dad for the day. You'll be fine. I'll be fine. I'll see you for supper tonight."

. . . .

CHAPTER FOUR

TAKING MY ACT ON THE ROAD

To be smart is to know that I love you.
To be wise is to feel my love
even when you're away.

Bouncing Baby Billy wanders away from Mom to explore a new environment, checking back visually. Is Mommy still there? Am I okay? Mom's smile and dramatic wave from across the room reassures. She communicates without words, "You're safe. I'm watching."

This is magic. Just months ago the same child needed to be held to feel reassured. He needed the immediacy of touch, Mommy's familiar smell, and the deep muscle reassurance of being held to calm. To settle. And now magic happens: Somewhere in the course of development, he's become able to get this same reassurance remotely. It's not Wi-Fi. He's developed the capacity to carry Mommy-love around in his head.

This magic is called "internalization": making something not-me into part of me. Internalization can be conscious and intentional, as when a child wants to be just like an all-star athlete or a movie star hero. It's often documented in baby books and shared through social media among relatives when a child dresses up to look just like Mommy or Daddy.

Internalization is the culprit to blame when you look in the mirror and see your parent looking back. Not the genetic stuff like eye color and the shape of the nose, but those quirky traits and unique mannerisms that you associate with your mom or dad. The particular way that you lean your head to one side. The way you furrow your brow or stand or sit or laugh. We osmose our anchors' behaviors and attitudes and beliefs spontaneously the way that a sponge absorbs water.

We do this unconsciously in the process of defining self—determining the boundaries that distinguish me from not-me. We take pieces of our emotional anchor within to help us let go. Internalization packs up the important stuff and makes it portable, so we can move away from our emotional anchors while hanging on to the security they've provided us. We become better able to calm and reassure and nurture ourselves when we're carrying inside ourselves a piece of the person who once did that for us.

We can facilitate this sort of portable security in our kids by creating transitional objects.

Transitional Objects

These are symbols that represent the child's emotional anchor in its absence. They are pieces of Mom (or Dad or Grandpa) magically vested with powerful emotional meaning. A transitional object allows Baby Billy to let go and to go farther, confident that he's carrying something that makes him feel held tight.

When that toddler wanders away to explore a new environment, looks back, and is reassured by Mom's voice and dramatic wave, he's associating those two symbols—her voice and the gesture—with the comfort and security she provides. That's the magic. It is compacting actual safety and nurturance into something remote and abstract. This ability means that the child can begin to manage longer and greater separations.

Transitional objects allow us to feel like we're being held tight even while we're letting go. They are the hand that we imagine holding while we cross the street; and the water wings we wear when we first let go of the side of the pool. They are the lockets and amulets and keepsakes that remind us of home; the extra dose of medicine, spare tank of gas, and just-in-case change of clothes we may never need but we keep on hand anyway.

Children often spontaneously create their own tangible transitional objects. Mommy's scarf or Daddy's watch or a special blankie serve as an invisible umbilical cord, carrying an absent parent's felt-love and easing the transition from holding tight to letting go.

Transitional objects tend to become smelly and filthy over time. They may be plainly disgusting to anyone but the child who carries them. Though worn out by overuse, torn, and mangled, they are irreplaceable and too precious to risk washing or scrubbing. They are as well-loved as *The Velveteen Rabbit*[1] and just as proud. All good sense and hygiene aside, the scars and the dents and the smell become part of the object's magic.

Anything associated with a loved one can become a transitional object. Special pieces of clothing or jewelry are common choices. The most powerful transitional objects communicate to our least mature senses: smell and taste and texture. The synthetic fur of a stuffed animal. A handkerchief or scarf that carries the scent of a parent's cologne or perfume. The shape and taste of a particular pacifier, food, or drink.

Visual and auditory associations demand more sophisticated cognitive processes—more thinking. A handwritten note from Mom, a special photo, or an audio or video recording can each work as a transitional object for a more mature child. These have the advantage of being more socially acceptable among the child's peers than a pacifier or a stained and stinky stuffed animal, but may be less emotionally evocative.

Hum a Happy Tune

Transitional objects may be most powerful when they are tangible, but tangibles are also losable and take-away-able. When a disorganized and forgetful child risks misplacing a treasured friend or an uninformed caregiver risks punishing the child by removing a transitional object, music can help.

---

1. Margery Williams, *The Velveteen Rabbit* (New York: Doubleday, Doran, and Company, 1922). Also check out *The Kissing Hand* by Audrey Penn (Terre Haute: IN: Tanglewood Press, 1993) for another excellent children's book relevant to transitional objects.

You and your child can share a favorite song or a made-up tune that anchors you to one another. When he's scared or worried, he hums it to feel closer to you. It's not a secret to be kept from others (because we know that secrets can be destructive), but it also can't be lost or taken away.

Adults, too, rely on transitional objects no less than children, although usually in more subtle ways. Take inventory right now, right here as you're reading. Chances are that you have something that subtly and privately connects you to the emotional anchors in your life. For example, you might wear lockets or rings or carry old photos. These objects help us hold on to pieces of our parents and grandparents and lovers after they're gone. They provide comfort in their absence.

If you were stuck in an elevator in the dark, locked down in a terrorist threat, or trapped inside your disabled car, your first move would be to do something practical. Call 9-1-1. Stop the bleeding. Try to escape. But as the ordeal continued, you'd look for emotional support.

What would you do to calm yourself? To feel reassured?

In the absence of real contact with a loved one, you might find yourself fiddling unconsciously with your wedding ring or distracting yourself with pictures of family members. You might find comfort in the idea that your mother gave you the shirt that you're wearing or that your daughter gave you the tie around your neck last Father's Day.

Of course, cell phones have changed the need for transitional objects dramatically and, in the process, have begun to redefine the whole idea of holding on and letting go. Not many years ago, a crisis usually meant coping alone—managing both the practical and the emotional necessities of the moment by yourself until help arrived. Before cell phones became as universal as pocket change, we were forced to rely on symbolic means of connecting with absent loved ones during a crisis. Immediate voice-to-voice and video connections have greatly diminished the need for symbolic umbilical cords. Why bother with a blankie if you can talk to Mom directly?

It's impossible to say whether this is a change for the better or the worse. On the one hand, if I have to be stuck in an elevator or locked down in a terrorist threat, I'd much rather speak to my wife and kids directly than have to comfort myself looking at the faded and crumpled photos I carry in my wallet. And if my daughter was anxious and alone and far away, I'd much rather FaceTime or Skype with her than leave her to find comfort in the locket I gave her for her birthday.

But as a psychologist, I can't help but wonder how human development might be altered when internalization is made obsolete by instant global access. We know, for example, that the brains of children who learn to read using computers are different from the brains of children who learn to read books on paper.[2] What we're yet to learn is whether the homesick fourth-grader who calls home for comfort in the midst of a midnight thunderstorm while he's at camp is missing out on a critical growth opportunity. He's likely to be comforted more easily and more completely by talking to his mom miles away, but if he doesn't learn to comfort himself this time, will he be able to the next time? If technology allows us to feel held tight always and everywhere, how will we ever learn to let go?

SHIFTING BOUNDARIES

It's ironic, perhaps, to think that the proliferation of material things—cribs and car seats and bassinets and walkers and even the idea that a baby should have her own room—has increased the physical boundaries between people, even while the proliferation of digital technology decreases our emotional boundaries. We are becoming more physically distinct but less emotionally so. Chapter 20 anticipates this evolutionary trend and its impact on parenting today.

Transitional Affiliations

Proximal (nearby, close-at-hand) symbols of security suffice during early development; think of Mom's wave and bright smile across the

---

2. Nicholas Carr, *The Big Switch: Rewiring the World, from Edison to Google* (New York: W. W. Norton & Company, 2008).

room. Tangible representations of security get us through childhood; these are the blankies and lockets and photos. And layered upon these are the teenager's transitional affiliations.

An affiliation is a connection with a group, club, or association of some kind. It could be as obvious and concrete as a membership to the local gym or as subtle and personal as a wish to be like a rock star. In the teenage years, affiliations are often advertised loud and clear on T-shirts and posters featuring beloved bands and teams and public figures.

Letting go is a gradual process at best. Two steps forward and one step back. The toddler wanders off but then returns to Mommy's lap. The third-grader goes on a field trip for one day. The middle schooler leaves for summer camp scared but comes back exhausted, filthy, and begging to return. While transitional objects help children take these steps by making their emotional fuel portable, transitional affiliations represent the teenager's first efforts to find emotional fuel away from home.

Transitional affiliations are oases that make crossing the desert that lies between childhood and adulthood possible. They are to our children what the space station is to astronauts: Exhausted by the effort necessary to escape Earth's atmosphere, explorers rest and refuel at the space station before venturing farther into the unknown. Transitional affiliations validate and communicate belonging. Membership in a group says, "I'm not alone." They become secondary emotional anchors during the turbulent process of defining identity and relatedness as our children try to balance holding tight and letting go.

A transitional affiliation is a real or imagined connection with a group outside of home. The group might be formally organized and recognized, like a church youth group, a Scout troop, or the school football team. It might be organized but unofficial, like a neighborhood clique, a garage band, or a gang. Or it might be diffuse, without organization or community recognition, the way that some teenagers will refer to themselves as "jocks" or "geeks" or "preppies."

And it might not even be real.

Adolescence means significant developments of both body and

mind. Less obvious than the growth spurts, acne, and cracking voices is the teenager's emerging capacity for abstraction and fantasy. A new depth of imagination opens the door for consideration of alternate realities, for science fiction, for torrid romance, and for affiliations that are partly or wholly make-believe.

The Internet capitalizes on teenagers' newfound capacity for fantasy. Facebook's introduction of "friending," groups built around Instagram pages and Pinterest accounts, and even the more formal networks created on LinkedIn, allow us to feel connected even if we never meet face-to-face. Video games take this one step further. MMORPGs (massive multiplayer online role-playing games) create virtual communities of real people disguised as avatars who work together to create wholly imagined worlds. Strangers meet to conduct shared digital quests to defeat dragons, accumulate wealth, construct fortresses and win competitions. Today, these virtual communities serve as transitional affiliations for many teens the same way that sororities, fraternities, and gangs did in generations past.

Yet digital affiliations confuse and concern many parents. The abrupt cultural shift from hanging out in a crowd to hanging out in the cloud strikes many moms and dads as bizarre and threatening. It used to be that we actually met our children's friends from time to time. We could monitor—if not actually choose—the groups with whom our teenagers affiliated.

The bad news is that the Internet makes this less and less likely. Horror stories abound. For this reason, parents are well advised to provide Internet access only on the condition that children will have no privacy.

The good news is that there is no such thing as a secret transitional affiliation.

The whole purpose of adolescent group affiliation—whether it's the soccer team or a cult—is to declare your identity loud and clear, to declare your belonging. The message is, "I feel secure and confident because my homies have my back." That's why gang members wear colors. Scouts and athletes wear uniforms. Fraternities and sororities have Greek letters on pins and pendants. Nerds dress differently from geeks who dress differently from preppies. Halo devotees and GTA (Grand Theft Auto) aficionados and Minecraft players speak distinct languages. Pokemon players eschew Yu-Gi-Oh! players and both look down upon DnD (Dungeons and Dragons) players. All of these are as obvious to the casual observer as a bird's species is to an ornithologist.

Corporate America knows this best of all. Branding sweatshirts and sneakers (er, sorry, "kicks"); T-shirts and caps, and notebooks and lunch boxes is a multi-billion dollar industry. What this means most concretely is that it often takes only a glance to identify a teenager's affiliations, likes, and dislikes.

Facilitated Letting Go

Transitional objects and transitional affiliations often emerge and disappear spontaneously over the course of development, taking on tremendous meaning for a period and then falling into disuse. A one-eared, coffee-stained, stuffed Dalmatian is a three-year-old's must-have companion at bedtime but, months later, is just another among a hundred torn and tattered plush pets. A first-grader refuses to leave the house without Dad's broken wristwatch, but by second grade the treasure has been replaced by a hat featuring a superhero character. A twelve-year-old seems to eat and drink and breathe the local football team. He wears the team's jersey, carries the players' trading cards, and rambles off their statistics like a Vegas bookie, until he becomes smitten with the red-head in math class.

Each of these transitional objects and affiliations serves as a child's emotional umbilical cord, connecting him or her to a psychological anchor. They are each a step toward internalizing security and confidence. The tattered Dalmatian and the broken watch and the symbols of the football team emerged spontaneously to help each child better cope with letting go.

When we understand how transitional objects and affiliations work, we can use them to help our kids better cope with anticipated stresses: Marital separation and divorce. Parent-child separations due to an adult's illness, surgery, military deployment, incarceration, or extended business travel. Anxieties associated with relocation, change of schools, remarriage, or the adoption of a sibling. These and a million other predictable stresses can often be eased by artificially introducing transitional objects and transitional affiliations.

Children who migrate between their parents' distinct and disparate homes are often forced to manage letting go too soon, too long, and too often. No matter how this child's schedule of care is crafted, she is always letting go.

Access to the absent parent via distance media can be one part of the solution. Cell phones and Skype and FaceTime; text messages; and Facebook and Twitter and Instagram can all create a digital umbilical cord—a means of feeling connected with one anchor even while living with another. But enabling and encouraging a child's digital contact with an absent parent has its risks as well. Batteries die. Cell coverage lapses. Schedules and punishments conflict with planned contacts.

Reliance on distance media may become a problem, for example, when the child uses the opportunity to disrupt the family's routine or to undermine a parent's authority. If Billy is entitled to call Dad while he is in Mom's care, he's likely to discover that he can use this artifice to avoid bedtime, delay leaving for school, and even to escape punishments.

Distance media can be unfulfilling to young and immature children who need taste and touch and texture contact to be emotionally refueled. These children often find phone and video chats little more than a distraction, sometimes prompting the absent parent to allege that the present parent is undermining the effort. At the other end of the spectrum, older and more sophisticated children may find FaceTime or Skype contacts with an absent parent fulfilling, but go on to abuse the privilege of unsupervised media access.

Compounding these issues are those situations in which distance media is impractical or impossible. A parent who is incarcerated, deployed, or terribly ill may not be able to Tweet wake-up greetings, bedtime wishes, or homework reminders across the distance. In these and similar situations, we can help children manage the anxiety of letting go via more conventional and concrete means:

- The simple fact is that we all smell. We don't like to think about it and we commonly try to camouflage it, but we each carry a unique scent. As infants, our kids recognize our scent long before they have words. They learn to associate it with the comfort we provide. With a little creativity, we can use this olfactory umbilicus to help our kids when we are apart: spray your familiar perfume or cologne on her bedsheets or a stuffed animal. Sleep in a favorite T-shirt several nights in a row, then send that unwashed shirt with her as a nightshirt or pillowcase. She may not even be aware that your scent is there, but she'll nonetheless be reassured.

- Write twenty, fifty, or a hundred brief, undated greetings: "Thinking of you" or "I love you" or "Remember our day at the beach?" (Try to avoid messages that communicate sadness and grief, like "I miss you.") Seal each in a separate envelope and leave the collection with the child's immediate caregiver (other parent, babysitter, nanny) to be delivered one by one, as needed, while you're apart.

- Create a "Mommy box" or a "Daddy box" with your son or daughter before the anticipated separation and leave it with the child. A shoe box will do. Tape the lid shut. Cut a slot in the lid. This is where the child will put the pebbles she finds and drawings she makes and notes she writes while you're apart, to be reviewed together upon your return. The box itself will serve as your proxy even if it remains empty, making your presence felt while you're away.

- Take a photo of you and your child together and tape it inside her school lunchbox or locker. Pose for pictures she can keep in her cell phone or print and post on her bedroom walls.

- Make yarn bracelets you can exchange or buy interlocking pendants that you'll wear.

- Consult with your child's teachers, clergy, school counselor, or therapist about other ways to support her while you're gone. Sometimes joining a support group will help.

Practical Pointer:

DIGITAL DUE DILIGENCE

Do you have a digital communications privacy contract with your kids? Brainstorm with them now and ask them to write the first draft. Structure the agreement around the answers to five questions:

1. Is the child ever entitled to privacy in any digital medium ever? Or should she expect that Mom and Dad are going to be looking over her shoulder, checking her phone, and censoring her access?

2. If she's allowed any degree of privacy, how is it defined? How can media privacy rights be earned or lost?

3. What can and should she share with others online (address, phone, name, age, social security number)? What must she never share with anyone online?

4. What should she do when she sees something confusing or disturbing online?

5. What can/should she do if she is aware that another child is engaged in a dangerous activity online?

· · · · · · · · · ·

CHAPTER FIVE

THE POWER OF ANXIETY

Worrying is
just one of the ways that
I make sure you never leave me

Don't make the common mistake of thinking that anxiety only means fear or worry.

Anxiety is like the pressure that fills a balloon. You must have some to be aware and alert and responsive to the world, but too much makes you fragile and explosive. Too little and you're bored and vulnerable. Too much and you're panicky. Fear, worry, and terror; panic and dread; and horror and alarm are only extreme states of what is otherwise a universal and necessary part of being alive.

Just as we are all innately motivated by the need for air and food, water and shelter, we are all innately motivated to optimize anxiety. This means that we seek stimulation when anxiety diminishes and we seek comfort and reassurance when anxiety overwhelms. You and I do this by turning the volume up or down, by isolating or engaging with others, by taking on or refusing new challenges.

I didn't learn this in a classroom or a textbook. I learned this while driving my family to New York City. It was a beautiful, clear summer day. The road was empty, the car was comfortable, the windows were down, the music was loud, and we were singing along. Everything was great until somewhere outside of the city, the sky darkened. Traffic jammed. Construction appeared. I was on an unfamiliar road among aggressive drivers in a downpour. My reaction? Without thinking, I turned off the music and asked my kids to stop singing.

Why did I do that?

My anxiety had escalated. I needed to get it under control. I'd become overwhelmed, so I instinctively controlled what I could. Less noise meant less distraction, which meant better focus on the road, which, in turn, meant less anxiety.

Not incidentally, my reaction also had an impact on my family. They heard my voice change. My words became abrupt. I'm sure that my posture became stiff. My anxiety fueled their anxiety like an echo, though they may not have known why they felt on edge.

This dynamic plays out over and over again in all of our lives. Each of us acts to control our felt-anxiety with echoes that impact others.

Now think about what happens when Mom and eighteen-month-old Bouncing Baby Billy enter an unfamiliar room together. Both feel anxious, and their feelings echo back and forth, each fueling the other. Baby Billy feels Mom's anxiety in her rapid heartbeat, her tense grip, her rapid and shallow breathing, and the tone of her voice, so he holds on tight. Mom feels him clinging. She hears him whimper, so she offers reassuring words. Maybe she hums a familiar tune.

With time, the setting becomes more familiar. Sights and sounds and smells that were foreign minutes before start to become interesting rather than threatening. Mom's quiet words calm herself and her son. Grips loosen. Anxiety diminishes. Billy first scans the room visually and then, beginning to get bored, squirms to get down. "I want to explore," he seems to say.

More comfortable herself, Mom sets the toddler on his feet at her side, watching him carefully. Letting him go. The pair make eye contact briefly before he toddles off. How far he goes will depend on a hundred details, but time and distance and incidental events (a stranger enters the room, an abrupt noise startles the child) will gradually pique either the child's anxiety or Mom's or both.

High anxiety means retreat. It signals that it's time to use coping mechanisms to try to let some air out of the balloon. Over time, Mom has developed lots of choices for handling her rising anxiety. She might distract herself with her cell phone. Or, she might practice her yoga mantra or the imagery and deep breathing techniques her therapist taught her. Bouncing Baby Billy has very few coping mechanisms, and they all amount to the same thing: retreat to his emotional anchor.

He may toddle back to Mom, crying. Or he might simply collapse on his well-padded bottom and cry, arms held out signaling a pick-up. He might offer a few words, but anxiety compromises more mature functioning so even a verbally precocious toddler is likely to say little. Either way, the message is the same: Hold me tight.

Back in Mom's arms, Billy's reassured. Refueled. He feels her heartbeat slow. Her breathing becomes regular. Her grip loosens. He hears her soothing words and gentle hum. These are the non-verbal signals that mean safety. There is no threat. Message received. Billy's own body relaxes. His anxiety decreases. The moment lasts until his anxiety drops too low, and then he squirms out of Mom's grip once again.

Let me go.

Hold me tight.

This back-and-forth, yo-yo-like dynamic will play out a million times during the years ahead. The setting will change and the distances will gradually increase, but the process will remain unchanged. The child gradually learns to regulate anxiety first by proximity to an emotional anchor, and later by proxy through transitional objects, and still later by affiliation with groups. Hold me tight; let me go. With each repetition, we internalize another grain of confidence. We take into ourselves the security associated with our mom and dad and grandma and coach and teacher and big sister and even Fido. Bits and pieces of these experiences accumulate like snowflakes, each insignificant but together gradually building an impressive mass. This is confidence, the internal means of managing anxiety.

FURRY ANCHORS?

Chapter 17 introduces some of the ways in which pets can become emotional anchors. Certainly, we know that some pets (especially dogs) are trained to assist people who are differently abled. But many people don't know that pets are being used more and more in professional settings to help people manage anxiety. In Ohio, for example, several jurisdictions provide "court dogs" to help children manage the anxiety that often arises when appearing in abuse, neglect, and family law matters. Some psychotherapists use dogs as part of their practice to help children feel comfortable and safe and to talk freely.

When the Anchor Isn't Secure

If every mom and dad and grandma and coach and teacher and big sister (and Fido) were 100 percent sensitive and responsive to every Billy and Sally in their lives, I'd happily be out of a job. If every human being had the benefit of at least one solid, reliable emotional anchor through childhood, Planet Earth would be a far healthier place.

The tragic reality is that nothing is ever 100 percent reliable, human beings least of all. We are flawed, imperfect creatures vulnerable to disease and addiction, exhaustion and confusion and need. We die. Compounding this is the fact that the necessary prerequisites for procreation have nothing at all to do with the social, emotional, and cognitive prerequisites for parenting. Said more simply: Selfish, immature, and emotionally ill people can have babies too.

Human imperfection means that the parent-child relationship is imperfect as well. The elegant holding-tight, letting-go dynamic that has evolved through millennia for the purpose of gradually building a child's self-sufficient and portable confidence, can fail and often does. Every one of us has at least occasionally tugged on an anchor rope in need of reassurance only to find that the emotional anchor is gone. Busy. Distracted. Unresponsive. Sick or drunk or high. Uncaring or dismissive. Unavailable or just plain absent.

When this happens in the teenage years, it's easy to retreat to earlier anchors. Fifteen-year-old Sally gets cut from the soccer team or rejected by her boyfriend. Her anxiety skyrockets. She's mad and sad and scared, so she digs Pooh Bear out of the closet. Pooh is stained, tired, and has lost an eye, but his scruffy fur and special scent are comforting There was a time when Pooh went everywhere with Sally, but now he's taken out of retirement only on special occasions.

And Dad is there to give Sally a hug. He's cautious, because he's learned the hard way that teenagers sometimes reject physical affection, but he reads her face and opens his arms. He takes her out for ice cream or just sits with her, even if nothing is said.

Just as Bouncing Baby Billy ventured across an unfamiliar room and, startled, cried for reassurance, Sally finds comfort too. Having been let go, she is once again held tight.

But what if the anchor isn't secure from the start? What if the newborn fails to discover that distress leads to holding? What if the toddler wanders off and, anxious, turns back but Mom's no longer there?

The answer should be as obvious as it is heartrending. If a secure emotional anchor means that a child can learn to manage his own anxiety and grow toward confidence, then the experience of an insecure emotional anchor can mean that anxiety grows unchecked and confidence remains elusive.

The results are startling to see, and they illustrate how incredibly adaptable we human beings really are. Imagine that Baby Billy has learned over time and experience that his mom often won't respond to his tears. She might be an addict or depressed or exceedingly self-involved. At fifteen months old, Billy doesn't know why and he doesn't care. The same way that you've learned over time that a particular chair in your living room is fragile so you don't sit on it, Billy has learned over time that he can't rely on Mom, so he makes different choices.

Now put mother and child in the middle of a room they've never before encountered. New smells and sounds and sights pique the child's anxiety. Billy's instincts tell him to retreat to his emotional anchor for comfort, but his experience tells him that Mom won't respond. She's already on her phone, ignoring him.

Mom might set Billy down before he's ready or resist his efforts to be released. Knowing she's likely to be too distracted to meet his gaze as he wanders off, Billy doesn't bother to look back. When he is startled by an abrupt sound, Billy's anxiety skyrockets. He collapses on his (squishy, as his needs aren't being met) bottom crying, but makes no gesture for pick-up. Why bother? History has taught him it's not coming. He may even resist Mom if she does pick him up.

Meanwhile, Mom may have no idea how she has contributed to this dynamic. She finds her little boy's squirming, fussing, and rejecting behaviors challenging, at best, and more likely aggravating. She might respond harshly, yelling or even hitting, and/or by withdrawing further. She's likely to see Billy as having a problem and is at very high risk of creating a self-fulfilling prophecy.

How does this illustrate adaptability? Watch the same child in the same situation the very next day with Dad, rather than Mom, and see the difference. Time has taught the toddler that Dad is sensitive and responsive to his needs. Dad reads the child's hold-me-tight and let-me-go signals just right. When anxiety hits, Billy expects that Dad will be there to reassure him so he toddles off, startles, collapses on his (clean and dry and freshly powdered) bottom, crying, arms up for rescue and there's Dad. Reassuring. Refueling. Holding him tight. His heart rate slows. Breathing evens out. Muscles relax. Then Billy's off again.

Same child. Same physical setting. Distinctly different behaviors reflecting distinctly different experiences of care.

Here's the good news: Studies of children who have survived horrific trauma teach us that having at least one secure emotional anchor through it all can be enough. Home might be abusive and neglectful, but if every Sunday noon, like clockwork, here comes Grandma—kind and attentive and loving, sensitive and responsive—that one constant anchor may be sufficient. And, of course, that anchor need not be Grandma specifically. A neighbor or teacher or coach, a therapist or sibling or even Fido, everyone's proverbial best friend, might do the trick

REMEMBER YOUR EMOTIONAL ANCHORS?

One steady, constant anchor can be enough. We are a resilient species, able to grow toward health with only the barest emotional nutrients.

Who was your emotional anchor growing up? Recalling the profound reassurance of being held by that person now will help you think differently about the way that you interact with your own child. Focus on being an emotional anchor, and leave the teaching to the teachers. Pick your battles. Make it a point to simply be present and in the moment with your child at some point every day.

For example, I often ask families to build block towers together. Some parents instruct their children what to do and how to do it to create a Frank Lloyd Wright–worthy construction, but at what cost? Other parents ask their kids what they think, experiment with their suggestions no matter how silly, laugh when the effort collapses, and then try again. I'd gladly hire the first—the product-oriented parents—to build my next home. I'd gladly hire the second—the process-oriented parents—to care for my children.

Here's more good news: Even children raised in insensitive, unresponsive emotional environments who don't have a doting grandma in the background can be okay anyway. Later childhood experiences of sensitive and responsive care can help (if not entirely correct) earlier insecurities. This observation is critically important when considering adoption. Except in those most grievous instances of long-term, early institutional neglect resulting in reactive attachment disorder, many children can use their later experiences of holding tight and letting go to learn how to appropriately control their anxiety.

THE CIRCLE OF SECURITY®

Attachment researchers have pioneered an intervention called the Circle of Security® to (re-)train parents to respond to their children in more sensitive and responsive ways and thereby enhance attachment security. The program, which uses video feedback, is very educational, supportive, and successful. It illustrates two important points about holding tight and letting go, one more obvious than the other:

1. Parents can be taught to hold tight and let go with their children even if they never had the experience themselves. Using visual and auditory cues captured and reviewed on video, parents can learn to better interpret and respond to their children's unique needs.

2. As with any successful psychotherapy (see chapter 17), the quality of the trainer's relationship with the participating parent is critical to the success. Feeling held tight and carefully, cautiously let go, benefits parents which, in turn, improves their parenting and serves their children's well-being.

Practical Pointer:

LEARNING TO MANAGE ANXIETY

Whether anxiety is a passing reaction to stressful circumstances or a genetic predisposition, psychologists commonly recommend one or more of three simple methods to help get it under control:

1. Conscious breathing. Making the reflex action of inhaling and exhaling a practiced skill can help you to calm yourself. Purposefully slowing down your breaths makes many people feel more in control and helps to diminish signals that might otherwise amp the body up as if a real threat exists. We do this by learning to take in a deep breath slowly through our mouths, holding it for a silent count of three, and then releasing it slowly and fully through our noses. In . . . 1, 2, 3 . . . out.

2. Imagery. Pick a place that feels calm, safe, and familiar. For some that means sitting in a bedroom or a beach or a park bench; for others, that means floating in a boat on quiet water. Talk through the full sensory experience. What are the sounds, smells, tastes, textures, and sights associated with the place? Practice going there in your imagination, experiencing all of the senses so that the calm and security associated with the place returns.

3. Progressive muscle relaxation. Breathing and imagery can be difficult for some and even produce anxiety for others. A third alternative involves purposely tensing, holding, and then releasing muscle groups one at a time, from the toes up to the scalp. Do this yourself, lying in a comfortable and safe place, working your way up your torso: "tighten your belly muscles, hold that, now let it go . . . tighten your chest muscles, hold that, now let it go." Each muscle group will feel more relaxed after the exercise, causing your body to communicate safety and relaxation to your mind.

Of course, none of these methods can be learned when panic hits. They each have to be practiced and perfected routinely so that the skill is ready and available when it's needed. Try teaching your kids one or more of these methods each night before sleep.

· · · · · · · · · ·

CHAPTER SIX

THE MEANING OF MAD

My rage is a declaration of me-ness.
It's an effort to reject you
that I pray will never succeed.

If anxiety is the rope that connects child and anchor, anger is one of the tools that stretches the rope to new lengths. Done right, anger helps parent and child to let go. Anxiety helps them reconnect. Anger creates a more-or-less temporary, more-or-less painful physical and emotional distance that screams "me" and "not me."

The back-and-forth, yo-yo effect of holding tight and letting go that spans our lifetimes and describes our relationships can be plotted across time as a series of angry conflicts and remorseful reconciliations. The anger says, "Let me go." The reunion says, "Hold me tight." In this way, anger is not just normal but completely necessary.

Of course, anger gets a bad rap.

I guess that makes sense: Our world is so full of angry people committing horrific acts of violence that we mistakenly equate the two. While it may be that all violence is sparked by anger, it is not at all true that all anger leads to violence.

Our job as parents is to teach our children that the experience of anger is healthy and acceptable; that what matters is how the emotion is expressed. We do this with our words, but more so by example.

How do you express anger? Do you hide from conflict in sleep or substances or media addictions, pretending nothing happened and that the emotion doesn't exist? Do you hold your frustrations behind gritted teeth until the accumulated rage explodes volcano-like? Do you snap at every little thing? Or do you acknowledge the experience safely and constructively, with words?

Too many parents spend far too much time telling their children what *not* to do with their anger ("Stop hitting your sister!" or "Don't break your toys!"), and far too little time teaching them what is okay to do with frustration, anger, and rage. Write in a diary? Call a friend? Hit a pillow? Yell in the backyard? Run around the block? Is it okay in your home to stomp up the stairs? To slam a door? To curse under your breath? To call names? To run away?

CONTAINING STRONG FEELINGS

My favorite anger expression tool is an empty plastic milk jug. (Emphasis on *empty*.) Put one in the corner of the room and call it the family's "feelings jug."

Angry? Go over and scream in it, try to crush it. Throw it at the wall. Stomp on it. Milk jugs are marvels of physics. With the cap snapped or screwed on firmly, they're nearly indestructible. Designate use of the feelings jug as an acceptable outlet for strong feelings like anger so that no one gets hurt. Nothing is damaged. Don't forget, your children will do what you do long before they do what you say. This means that you, too, need to use the feelings jug. Smash it; then come back better able to talk about what made you so mad. You're just going to recycle it anyway.

And just as important: How is anger resolved in your home? After an angry incident, do you just wake up the next morning, make breakfast, and go off to school or work, pretending that nothing happened? Do you carry a grudge for days, giving one another the silent treatment long beyond the time that you remember what you were mad about? Or do you take just enough time to cool off, and then sit down and talk it through?

If your adult conflicts are loud and scary, but your apologies are secrets hidden behind closed doors, how will your kids ever learn to apologize? You can always demand, under threat of punishment, that your children utter an apology, but those words will be empty of meaning and the idea of apologizing and reconciling—letting go and then coming back and holding tight—will become just as hollow if they have never witnessed you apologizing yourself.

At no time is this lesson more obvious and painful and destructive than when children learn that anger ends love. Mom and Dad fight. The conflict might build over weeks or months or years, or it may erupt suddenly, volcanic and terrifying, in a single day. It might be subtle or even silent—rage expressed in wordless scowls, profanities texted across the dinner table, with backs turned. The ritual kiss good-bye or the hug goodnight is purposely forgotten. Or the conflict might be loud, rationalized in the foolish belief that the kids are asleep and won't hear, or that they're playing video games and won't see. Worse still, the kids might be drawn into the fray, asked to play messenger ("Tell your mom that I won't be home") or forced to choose sides ("Do you want to go with him or with me?").

This is not about marriage or divorce. Those are formalities important to city hall, the IRS, and the courts. What matters to your kids is that their anchors are being uprooted. Their security is coming undone. A child who sees anger end love may ever after fear that anger is destructive and unacceptable.

This child has learned that anger means letting go. Period. There is no return to holding tight.

Anger is *not* the opposite of love.

We must teach our children that anger can erupt and be resolved within the safe container of love, no different from happiness, sadness, or fear. Anger need not be scary or destructive or violent. Yes, it can be painful—any experience of letting go in any circumstance can be painful—but the pain will resolve. The anchor is secure. For every letting-go, no matter how loud and rageful, there must always be a corresponding holding-tight.

These lessons may be most obvious during the mythic "terrible twos" and during that excruciating period we call adolescence, but in truth they occur every day across the full span of our lives. Little annoyances, aggravations, and frustrations erupt like waves on the ocean but are soon resolved or forgotten or are simply overwhelmed by the next wave. Larger upsets arise less often, sparking real anger, fury, or rage. These get screamed out or cried out in a tsunami of words and actions soon to be regretted and probably never meant in the first place. The worst of these are brought to a trusted relative or counselor or friend for assistance. Some are memorialized by a knuckle-shaped dent in the wall, a broken toy, or even a police record. But in healthy families all of these separations are sooner or later reconciled. Every "I hate you" is resolved in a tearful "I love you." Every experience of letting go comes back to holding tight.

Children must actively, assertively, often abrasively, and sometimes even violently let go. Push away. Separate. I would be gravely concerned about the well-being of a child who claimed never to have been mad at Mom or Dad. Anger happens. If we teach that anger means an end of love, it will go underground. It will be hidden and denied, until the pressure breaches the container, exploding in violence toward self or others.

Does this mean that anyone should tolerate abuse or acts of destruction or violence in their lives? Of course not. Start by teaching how to express frustration and anger and rage appropriately. Make the experience as normal as . . . well, come to think of it, the best analogy is sexual behavior.

The healthiest response to a child's emerging sexual explorations—from his earliest interest in body parts to his embarrassed adolescent cravings, questions, and experiments—is to reassure that the interest is healthy, to clarify what is acceptable ("Okay, but please do that in your room with the door closed. . . ."), and to be firm and clear about what is not acceptable. Anger is just as natural, just as provocative, and calls for exactly the same response. It's okay. Here's what is okay to do. Here's what's not okay to do. Period.

A Quick Lesson on the Development of Emotion

The newborn knows only two states: Comfort and discomfort. Sated and needy. Anxiety-diminished and anxiety-renewed. There is little or no distinction within these two essential states. There's no such thing as discomfort in my tummy but my legs feel okay. It's not, "I'm nervous about the stock market but happy with my savings." The newborn's experience is global and black and white. Comfort and discomfort are complementary opposites like the seats on a seesaw. As one goes up, the other goes down. A parent's job is to read and respond to the child's ups and downs, helping to define and fulfill needs. To regulate impulse and emotion.

Remember that unfulfilled need is a new experience for the child. Before birth, need and need fulfillment were seamlessly connected. The mother's body automatically regulated the child's state much the same way that a thermostat automatically regulates the temperature in the room you're sitting in right now. Too hot? Click. The air conditioner kicks in. Too cold? Click. The furnace fires up.

Birth breaks the thermostat. What once was communicated efficiently via hormones through the umbilical cord now must be communicated behaviorally across space and time. The parent is still in charge of regulating the child's anxiety, but no longer receives and responds to the child's signals automatically. New signals must be established. Sight and sound and movement, taste and texture and smell—all play a role in the newborn's efforts to express need and in the adult's efforts to read and respond accordingly.

Need arises spontaneously: Energy wanes and fatigue sets in. Food is digested causing bladder and bowels to fill and then release. Diapers become uncomfortable. The cute little sweater that Grandma sent chafes at the neck. Gas bubbles expand and contract. When need goes unfulfilled, even momentarily, anxiety erupts, fueling reflex physical tension. Muscles contract, limbs thrash, and cries emerge. This isn't yet communication. There's no intention or association. Just reflex. But when Mom sees and hears (and feels and smells) the result, she responds. She holds the child tight.

Later, when the baby calms, she lets him go. Sets him down.

This is the first brick in the foundation of the enormous structure that will become communication. Social language. Anxiety prompts holding tight. Diminished anxiety prompts letting go.

With this cornerstone in place, the rest of the building goes up gradually over decades, although never painlessly. Learning to interpret and respond to a newborn's unique signals can be both the most frustrating and rewarding process anyone can ever know. It's trial and error supercharged by hormones and played out on the field of community approval. A screaming and crying and thrashing baby is not only expressing discomfort, but also seems to be declaring that her caregiver is incompetent, thereby proving every new parent's worst fears.

How hard could it be? The choices are limited, after all. You know that she's not asking for cream in her coffee or a weather report. Does she need a new diaper? A bottle? Sleep? Are her socks too tight? When she finally settles ("Aha! You were hungry!"), you feel triumphant. You are momentarily rewarded and redeemed in your own eyes and in those of all who look on, the child herself most of all.

It helps that reducing the child's anxiety also reduces the parent's anxiety, a reward in and of itself. It also helps that babies are pretty good—but not perfect—little suckers. They invariably take in a lot of air when they drink. This air is expelled in one of two ways, one of which happens to turn up the corners of their mouths. Needy and exhausted parents see this reflex behavior and call it pleasure. Even gratitude. Mom feels successful, thinking she made the baby happy, so she smiles back. She rocks and coos and comforts the child.

Unaware that he smiled first, Bouncing Baby Billy quickly associates Mom's upturned lips and his own upturned lips with anxiety relief. Comfort. Need fulfilled. He learns to make this facial expression even in the absence of gas. Smile elicits smile, which is associated with feeling good. Happiness is defined. Relationship is renewed.

Now rewind and look at the sequence of events more closely: The experience of unfulfilled need creates the child's first experience of frustration in the form of delayed gratification. Unfulfilled need caused muscles to tense, resulting in thrashing and crying. Thrashing and crying made Mom magically appear and with her comes need fulfillment. Gratification.

Thrashing and crying worked. It resolved the problem.

We've implicitly taught the child to lash out.

This is anger in its most primitive state.

Don't worry: There's nothing wrong with feeding (or changing or comforting) a crying baby (and a lot wrong with not doing so). This feedback loop is self-correcting over time. As the child grows, the behaviors that worked in infancy gradually become unacceptable and even dangerous. A thrashing newborn gets picked up and comforted, his primitive communications rewarded. A thrashing ten-year-old gets put down and may be disciplined, his immature behavior labeled as unacceptable. A thrashing teenager risks being hospitalized or jailed. These social pressures shape how we learn to manage frustration and achieve gratification, none more powerfully than the experience of holding tight and letting go.

SHORT-TERM ESCAPE OR LONG-TERM SOLUTIONS?

Giving in will get you through the moment. It will make the tantrum go away, the crying stop, and might even get you a dose of praise and gratitude, hugs and kisses, but it inevitably makes the problem worse.

If you are depressed or addicted or distracted or simply exhausted, you are likely to respond to your child's needs in the moment with little thought of tomorrow. Don't.

Parenting while impaired in any of these ways is as bad as driving under the influence. Your reflexes are slowed. Your thinking isn't clear. You're making bad decisions.

Tell your kids that you need a break. Don't blame them, but do show them that you can take care of yourself. Make sure they know when you'll be back and who will take care of them in your absence. Tag a trusted parenting partner into the ring while you take a break. Then eat a meal, soak in a hot tub, call a friend, see your therapist. Your kids need you refueled so that you can refuel them, and they need to learn by your example that we're all human and that self-care is more than just okay. It's necessary.

Practical Pointer:

WHEN FEELINGS OVERWHELM THINKING

As emotion increases, mature functioning declines. Overwhelmed with feelings, we have little or no access to our impressive cognitive skills. Instead, we react impulsively and even physically, often creating dangerous situations.

It is difficult if not impossible to get someone who is enraged to talk or think clearly, and the effort can get you hurt. Don't bother. Talking and thinking come later, after the pressure is released at least a little bit. This can mean prescribing physical outlets that are safe. Crushing or throwing or shouting into an empty milk jug is one answer. What are others?

You have to decide what works for you. Here are some suggestions:

It can be very rewarding to crush and rip and shred old newspaper. No one gets hurt. When a child uses this outlet, cleanup can be a side-by-side opportunity to talk it through. The pressure's eased. Now words can help.

Play-Doh and similar products can be hit and crushed and squeezed. Don't stand over an angry child and watch. Join in. Share the moment and the frustration; then debrief together afterward.

Large pads of newsprint and preschool crayons (those fat crayons are pretty durable) are inexpensive and can be great outlets.

Scribble, scream, write, and then shred what you wrote.

A punching bag in the basement? A set of free weights for an older child? A treadmill? Make your choices carefully, but opportunities for any sort of exercise will serve the purpose. Physical outlets release the pressure and allow you to move on to talking about the issue.

. . . .

CHAPTER SEVEN

ON STRUCTURE
AND PARACHUTES

The better that I am held,
the freer I become.

Imagine that you're the mom, seated in the middle of an unfamiliar room with precious Bouncing Baby Billy on your lap. It might be a doctor's office or a new friend's living room. Baby Billy clings to you, anxious in the midst of the new sounds and smells and sights, but comforted by all that is familiar and reliable about you. You're his anchor and his thermostat. You reassure him and help to keep his anxiety in balance.

He reads you more clearly than you're reading this page. As your heartbeat and breathing slow, as your grip subtly loosens, as the tone of your voice relaxes and the pitch of your voice deepens, he is reassured. You've communicated safety to him, and you may not even know it. Calmed, he scans the room from his safe nest in your lap. His need to be held tight diminishes and is slowly replaced by a wish to be let go. Something colorful catches his eye, and he begins to fuss.

This place is safe, you think, so you set him on his feet with a kiss and a reminder, "Stay where I can see you."

By now we know what Billy does. He toddles off, checking back visually to make sure that his anchor is secure, gradually stretching the anchor line to its limits. He wanders and explores until he stumbles or startles or becomes overwhelmed, and then he retreats back to you for reassurance.

Holding tight. Letting go.

But what about you? You're more than just a passive port in the storm. You're an equal and active player in this drama. If a stranger or an animal enters the room, if Billy picks up something that you judge to be dangerous, or if he wanders too far, you yank on the anchor rope, reeling him back in. You call out a warning or a reminder or simply say his name, your tone and pitch and volume communicating your escalating anxiety. "Billy?" offered calmly, conversationally, is just a check-in. It's a benign request to share a smile and eye contact to reassure both of you.

"*Billy!*" loud and sharp, communicates anxiety. Danger. He knows from experience that the tone, pitch, and volume you've used means fear. He looks up and sees that you have moved forward on the chair, that your muscles are taut and your eyes are wide. These signals fuel his anxiety just as if he were still in your lap feeling your grip around him tighten, your heart begin to race, and your breathing become rapid and shallow. It doesn't matter that you're twenty feet or twenty miles apart. He startles. Drops the flamethrower or the live chainsaw or the butcher knife that he'd discovered amidst the Legos, and he either toddles back to you for reassurance or plops down, whimpering for a pick-up.

Hold me tight, he signals. Regulate me; I'm scared.

This is limit setting and consequence. Structure. This is elemental holding expanded beyond arm's length. It is containment in a room rather than just in your lap. With development and experience, words and postures and facial expressions begin to convey what only actual physical holding could communicate earlier in life.

Structure is the container that reduces the overwhelming complexity and confusion of the universe into manageable, bite-size chunks. If birth means giving up the utter and complete reassurance of the womb, and development means giving up the imperfect reassurance of Mom's arms, structure makes it possible to pack up reassurance and take it out for a spin. To explore farther and make independent choices with some reasonable confidence of safety.

Structure is the limit that you set when you cautioned Baby Billy to "Stay where I can see you." It is the smile of reassurance you offered when he responded to his name, and it is the pick-up you provided when he toddled too far. Structure is the physical and emotional container that holds Billy when you're apart, a container that he will slowly but inevitably internalize—for better or worse—to define self from within. This is the subjective state that distinguishes the drip from the ocean. It is the invisible, intangible, internal cohesion that we variously call emotional security, confidence, or self-esteem.

"Stay where I can see you" is the limit. It defines the length of the anchor rope. If Billy complies, there is a consequence: reward in the form of a smile. And if he goes too far: retrieval and perhaps scolding. Either way—smiling with pleasure or screaming in protest—the certainly of if-then, limit-consequence reassures him. He feels contained. Anchored. Held tight.

Structure means limits on behavior. Limits define which among an infinite number of choices are acceptable and which are not. Limits are enforced by their connection to meaningful consequences. Eat your vegetables and get dessert. Hit your sister and go to your room. Do your chores and get a dollar.

Crawl out of my sight and get picked up.

Structure also means boundaries that define space. Boundaries declare "mine," as opposed to "not mine," usually in concrete and visible ways. These are the two-dimensional lines and three-dimensional fences and gates, walls and doors, and windows that say what is in and what is out. Where to go and where not to go. Which spaces are yours and which are not. The duct-tape line dividing the twins' bedroom in two. The drawer labeled "Billy" as distinct from the drawer labeled "Sally." It's the imaginary bubble that defines personal space. The closed door on the bathroom and the sign on the bedroom door that reads "keep out!" complete with skull and crossbones.

And structure means routines that define time—sequences of events as defined by calendars and schedules and rituals. "A" comes before "B," which comes before "C." Monday is clarinet practice, Tuesday is soccer, and Wednesday is dance. Brush your teeth, eat your breakfast, and then leave for school. Supper, bath, story, and then lights out for bed. Homeroom and then algebra and then social studies and then lunch.

But don't create a structure without expecting it to be tested. We poke at the fabric that holds us to make sure we are safe. Secure. Held tight.

When we discover that the container is secure, that the fabric doesn't rip and that "then" always follows "if," we feel secure even if we're not happy. Even if we're enraged. Limits and boundaries and routines can aggravate and annoy and just plain piss people off. Knowing this as parents means that we must never set a limit without being prepared both to follow through with the promised consequence and to tolerate the resulting emotions.

HEALTH VERSUS HAPPINESS

This is critical to healthy parenting:

We must always choose health over happiness. A healthy child can find his own happiness. A child made happy at the cost of his health will only know to come back to you again and again to make him happy.

Prioritizing health means that anger is likely to erupt. That's okay. Your job isn't to make your kids happy; it's to help them learn how to manage their natural and necessary experiences. Anger is one of them.

Doing this means saying "no" and following through with consequences, enforcing boundaries, and maintaining routines. It means that your teenage son cannot stay up until midnight on a school night and your pre-teen daughter cannot wear makeup and everyone's cell phones are recharging in the kitchen at bedtime. It may mean that you are declared "unfair" (true) and "mean" (maybe) and the worst mother on the planet (completely false). Showing your kids that you can handle their rage is the first step in teaching them how to do the same.

This is where many parents try hard but fail. Limits are set, but follow-through is weak. When this happens—because the parent can't tolerate the child's expected emotions—roles become reversed. The child has taken charge, controlling the parent by threatening tears or rage or some similar upset. Whether this happens because the parent is fragile and can't take a stand or needs the child's praise and reassurance, or because the parent fears that the child is fragile and can't tolerate the upset, the outcome is the same. Not only is the limit forgotten, but the child comes to see emotion as overwhelming. Unacceptable. Threatening.

When we step over the line and nothing happens, anxiety leaks back in, refilling the balloon. This can happen quite quickly, feeling like the immediate, gut-wrenching flood of panic that comes on when you pull the rip cord at five thousand feet but no parachute appears. Or the anxiety can seep in at a slower pace: an initial rush of giddy exuberance—the "I got away with it!" happy dance—that slowly degrades as reality sinks in.

Uh-oh. Where's my parachute? Who's going to catch me?

The preschooler who toddles away from Mom to the end of his emotional anchor rope and then farther, out of Mom's sight and hearing, may be having a great time until he becomes tired or anxious or scared. He crashes down on his cushy bottom, anxiety blooming, and calls out for Mom. Hold me tight, he says. Regulate my anxiety for me because I can't do it alone. When Mom doesn't arrive, crisis ensues. That no-parachute-falling-fast panic sets in.

The same thing happens when the ten-year-old wakes up terrified by a nightmare, when the thirteen-year-old is first confronted by sex or drugs, when the sixteen-year-old totals the car, and when you or I answer the door to find police waiting.

Or answer the phone to be greeted by an IRS auditor.

Or look in a child's room and find her bed empty.

Enraged, your eleven-year-old packed his bags and ran away. Indignant and insulted and embarrassed over some inequity, he broke the anchor rope and rejected the anchor. His bed is empty. At first, freedom mixed with vengeance tasted pretty good. Until it didn't. Until the night became scary and he became hungry and exhausted and the cold set in. Now, for the first time in his life, he cries out in pain and no one is there to pick him up. To hold him tight.

Practical Pointer:

NEGOTIATING STRUCTURES

We are all more likely to comply with structures when we feel like we've been involved in their creation. This is as true for democracies as it is for your children and the way they behave in your home.

Practice a "voice, not choice" philosophy. There are many times when you can tell your kids that a decision has to be made and invite their input, reassuring them that their parents will make the final choice. This works with routine matters like bedtime and allowance as well as with punishments for specific offenses.

Asking a child what she thinks the consequence should be for her misbehavior is a maturity test for all involved. Many children will prescribe a consequence that is more severe than you might even consider.

And those other children who are focused on blaming others and minimizing their own consequences? Asking their opinions teaches you more about how they think. Respond to their inevitable "It's not fair" and "I hate you!" rages with calm follow-through.

CHAPTER EIGHT

OILING WHEELS BEFORE THEY SQUEAK

I'd rather eat like a gourmet,
but I will scavenge for scraps, if I must.
I'd rather drink from a clear mountain stream,
but I will lap at a puddle, if I must.
I'd rather win your praise,
but I will drink up your rage, if I must.

Expectable but not acceptable.

This is the distinction that we as parents must make over and over and over again. As much or as little as you are able to anticipate your child's choices, you don't need to approve of them. A hundred books and a dozen grocery store magazines and a gaggle of talk show hosts are all eager to tell you about the milestones of child development. We're reassured to know that most three-year-olds hit, that most eight-year-olds lie, and that just about every eleven- or twelve-year-old threatens to run away at some time. These things may be expectable, but they're clearly not acceptable.

We communicate what is acceptable to our children in two ways.

First and most powerfully by our examples. We must expect that our kids will do as we do far more often than they do what we say.

We also teach our children what is acceptable by setting limits and following through with consequences—rules that regulate behavior and contingent outcomes. Limits and consequences communicate to children a sense of feeling held. Contained. Together with the boundaries that help to manage physical space and the routines that help to manage time, limits and consequences regulate anxiety.

Our own as much as our children's.

Limits are simply expectations for behavior made simple and clear. In their best form, limits are positive and explicit prescriptions for success. "Use your words" or "Share your toys" or "Flush when you're done" are each positive limits. Unfortunately, limits are far more commonly expressed in the negative, dictating which choices are forbidden.

"Don't hit your sister."

"Don't yell in the house."

"No turn on red."

"Do not pass go. Do not collect two hundred dollars."

Negative limits are usually tied to negative consequences—punishments—as in, "If you hit your sister, I'll send you to your room." The threat may work, but if so, it's because Billy is scared. He's intimidated. He wants to avoid an outcome that he finds aversive (being sent to his room), but even more so, he wants to avoid disappointing his parent. Fear makes it clear what not to do, but—far more critically—negative limits fail to communicate how to succeed. How to get what he wants from his sister and how to get what he needs from Mom or Dad: Approval. Reassurance. Feeling held.

This is why spanking doesn't work. True, your kids may change their behavior to avoid the threat. They'll learn to be sneaky and get better at not being caught. But ultimately, spanking teaches nothing about how to succeed, only how to avoid pain and humiliation. Far from leading children to feel reassured and secure, any limit associated with fear undermines security and breeds anger and resentment.

By contrast, positive limits associated with desirable rewards build self-esteem and cooperative relationships. They teach children how to succeed and motivate choices that invite pride, affection, and opportunity. They communicate feeling held.

Mom says, "If you and your sister can get along, then you'll get gold stars on your chart." This limit (*if cooperate*) and consequence (*then sticker*) prescribe a positive path to success. It says, "We're going to separate now. You can choose what you do while we're apart. Here's how you will get held tight when we're back together." To be effective, the reward has to be meaningful to the child and, far more critically, the reward has to be associated with your positive emotion.

Gold stars and plastic trophies and stickers may be pretty and may even be coveted within a peer group, but they are meaningless in and of themselves. For that matter, the same is true of money. The dollar bill in your pocket is just a pretty piece of paper except for the fact that the people holding us—the government—has invested it with extra meaning. Rewarding children with material things can be effective—they may comply with the limit in order to earn the object—but if the reward occurs without your pride and affection, hugs and high-fives and genuine caring, all the child has learned is to value things.

Gold stars and stickers are a special kind of transitional object. Distinct from the teddy bears and blankies that we discussed earlier, the trinkets we use as rewards to motivate our children's choices are booster shots of love. This idea is important in anticipation of the question that always comes up when I talk about limits and consequences: "If I give my son a sticker every time he makes his bed, aren't I teaching him to become greedy and materialistic? Shouldn't he just make his bed?"

Yes and no.

Yes, we live in a very materialistic culture. You go to work in order to earn a paycheck. Stickers and trophies and certificates and allowances do teach kids to expect more of the same in the future.

But no, if the sticker is accompanied by your praise, its real function is to help your son internalize the structure that you've provided. First he'll make his bed to earn the sticker. Still later, the sticker will matter less than your smile of gratitude and the idea that he's helped out. Later, long after you're gone and the stickers are forgotten, he'll feel good about making his bed because the bed is made.

Unfortunately, our squeaky wheel society has twisted the idea of limits and consequences into something harsh and destructive.

"Squeaky wheel"? The old saying suggests that only the squeaky wheel gets the grease. Running a machine or raising a child in this way means that the wheels that turn quietly and smoothly are ignored. Taken for granted. Only the wheels that wobble and make noise will get oiled. Sadly, this is how our society works far too often. Our health care system, for example, is an unwieldy and convoluted bureaucracy built to fix problems, with little or no investment in avoiding them in the first place. The system does little to reward your efforts to quit smoking, eat healthy, and lose weight, and instead devotes enormous resources to treating lung cancer and fighting obesity.

The size of the system doesn't matter. Whether we're talking about the United States of America or the father and son who live next door, the dynamics are the same. Positive limits paired with desirable rewards breed success, cooperation, and pride. Negative limits paired with threats of punishment breed conflict and competition, often leaving only the squeakiest wheel to get the oil.

In many cases, this is exactly what we've allowed to happen to our families.

You need to pass a test to become a plumber or an accountant; to own a firearm, drive a car, or fly a plane. In most states, you need a license just to go fishing. But all it takes to have a child are hormones, genitalia, and a partner.

Our culture provides very few positive limits and rewards to new parents in the interest of raising healthy children—improving the health and well-being of the next generation. Instead, we wait for the wheel to squeak. We neglect the opportunity to invest in prevention in favor of draining our very limited resources on repairs.

I have often advocated an alternative: Repeal the automatic federal dependent care tax deduction. Create a developmentally attuned series of Continuing Parent Education (CPE) courses and post them online so that parents can complete them in the comfort of their own home. When they do, they receive a certificate to file with their annual tax return that entitles them to claim the dependent care deduction. Those parents who don't complete the CPE courses wouldn't qualify for the dependent care deduction. The extra money they would pay in taxes would fund the whole program.

Limit and positive consequence: "If you complete a course and if you submit a CPE certificate, then you save money."

Limit and positive consequence: "If the government created a program of this sort, then our children would be healthier."

Simple, obvious logic: "If our children are healthier, the costs associated with special education, drug rehabilitation, crime, and health care, to name just a few critical social ills, would decrease, freeing up more resources and encouraging further investment in our children's futures.

Squeaky Wheel Parenting

Just as children internalize the structures that hold them, adults do the same. Living in a society that moves from one crisis to the next, feasting on a 24/7 diet of trauma and drama fed directly to your desktop and laptop, smart phone and watch, carried in the very air that we breath, it's easy to become a squeaky wheel parent.

Overwhelmed, angry, depressed, and distracted parents may take their children's successes for granted. Healthy choices and compliance, responsibility and maturity are ignored. When rewards are offered, they are offered devoid of emotion, breeding dependence on external rewards (materialistic stuff) and a general failure to grow toward internalized pride and motivation.

The result is a child who has no sense of being held, a child who is almost as excited as he is terrified to realize he's on his own. No one's watching. It's as if Bouncing Baby Billy, having toddled away from Mom, gets nervous and looks back for reassurance only to find that he's been forgotten. Mom is there, but she's too busy to look up. The eye contact and smile of reassurance that he needs to keep going is nowhere to be found. He's on his own to try to manage his anxiety.

But if Baby Billy gets hurts and cries? If he spills a drink on the floor? If he breaks a toy or interrupts a call or wanders off where he doesn't belong? Then Mom drops what she's doing and rushes in. Now she's supercharged with adrenaline (and perhaps a drop or two of guilt), and her upset fuels the child's upset. She is neither anchor nor thermostat; neither reassuring nor regulating the child's emotions. To the contrary, her anxiety floods the child, communicating terror, stoking the flames of his distress. Worse, because she's unaware how her emotions are feeding Billy's emotions, she's likely to misread the situation and overreact.

Now imagine the same dynamic played out across a lifetime. School success earns a glance. School failure is reason for meetings and testing and tutors and medication. Social successes—prom queen or king, class president, team captain—are ignored, but antisocial acts make everyone interrupt their latest Tweets.

A destructive kind of inflation occurs over time in squeaky wheel environments, as only the wheel that squeaks loudest gets the oil. Today, Billy's tantrum gets attention. Tomorrow, Suzie's school refusal steals Billy's thunder. Next week, Billy wrecks his car, but a month after that, Suzie reveals that she's been cutting her wrists. Mom and Dad's shock and horror are then trumped yet again when Billy shows up at school with a firearm.

Game. Set. Match.

Please don't misunderstand me: None of these crises are trivial or ever simply and solely the result of a pathological competition to squeak the loudest and earn a parent's attention. Each act likely has its roots in deeper conflicts, neurochemical differences, and traumatic histories. But each of these choices began with problems that might have been recognized earlier and might have been diminished or even avoided altogether if Mom and Dad had oiled the wheels before they squeaked. To anchor their kids as they toddled off, to collect them when they'd gone too far, and to help them learn to manage their own upset. To hold them tight and let them go, and then hold them tight again.

Accidental Rewards and Unintended Punishments

When twelve-year-old Billy showed up in math class without his homework for the third day in a row, his teacher sent him to the vice principal's office. The vice principal called Billy's mom and dad. Mom and Dad left work, drove across town, and squeezed into the administrator's cubbyhole office. The three adults crowded over Billy, confused and scolding and angry. Together, they made it clear that he was grounded in both homes and would be supervised while doing his homework every night.

All was well for a couple of days, and then Billy once again came to class unprepared. He had done his homework under Dad's strict oversight the night before, but he refused to turn it in. Tutors were hired, testing was ordered, and Billy was enrolled in psychotherapy where someone finally took the time to listen. As it turned out, Billy completely understood the limit: If he didn't do his homework and deliver it to the teacher on time, then he would have no electronics in either home.

Billy told his therapist that he cared very much about Facebook and Twitter and Xbox and TV, that he felt like he was invisible if he didn't have his cell phone, but he fairly glowed with excitement about the reward he knew he'd get for *not* doing his homework.

Reward?

REWARD SUCCESSES RATHER THAN WAIT TO PUNISH FAILURES

Of course you recognize that this is a squeaky wheel situation. The only identified outcome is negative and associated with failure. The vice principal would probably have been better off to create a positive contingency. For example: When you've turned in five homework assignments on time, you'll get fifteen minutes to shoot hoops in the gym at lunch. In this case, it's important that the contingency not require five successes in a row—you want to avoid a situation in which the child succeeds four times but earns nothing when he fails on day five.

"Yes," he said, "my parents got together and they agreed on something! It was pretty cool."

This reaction highlights not only how strongly we crave the feeling of being held tight by our caregivers—for Billy this meant his divorced parents' cooperation to meet his needs—but also the importance of the subjective impact of a contingency. Indeed, the meaning of a presumed reward or punishment is in the eye of the beholder. Until you know what a child values, the limits and contingencies you provide will be shots in the dark. Of course, some guesses are better than others. Preschoolers enjoy shiny trinkets featuring favorite media characters. School-age kids can become obsessed with sports heroes and celebrities. Teenagers often value access to devices that connect them with one another. Money matters to some, but not to others.

Sending a child to his room may be intended as a punishment when, in fact, the child relishes the opportunity to spend time away from the family drama surrounded by preferred objects. An early bedtime can be a powerful threat to many children, but an equally powerful reward to others.

The best way to avoid these inadvertent outcomes is to involve your child in creating the structures that hold her. The limits may be non-negotiable, but the rewards and punishments can be open to discussion. Try this: Brainstorm together to create a list of everything (tangible stuff and opportunities and privileges alike) that your child wants. No holds barred. Write each item on a separate note card. When you're done, discard the impossible and impractical things. To ride the space shuttle. To own a car. A trip to France. Then ask her to put the remaining cards in order from most desired to least. Would she rather earn a pizza party with a friend or download a new song by her favorite artist? Would she rather download a new song or be excused from taking out the trash for a week? Now assign expectations to rewards, making her most desired rewards hardest to earn.

The limit is: Make your bed before school without a reminder. Every success earns a poker chip. A trip to the mall costs three poker chips. A trip to the beach costs twenty poker chips. A trip to Disney costs three thousand. A plan of this sort not only assures that she values the rewards that you offer; it also teaches your child to tolerate frustration, delay gratification, and makes success on any scale a matter of shared pride. She will tell you whether she's ready to be let go for three days or three hundred days before she needs you to hold her tight.

One Final Word about Limits and Consequences

The motivational value of any outcome depends in part on its scarcity. No one would work to earn money if money really did grow on trees (although there would be a lot more trees). In the same way, it's important to think about whether the rewards you use to motivate your children are scarce enough to be valued.

Expecting your daughter to make her bed before school each day in order to earn a token that can add up to a trip to the mall or the beach or Disney will fail—even though she chose the rewards, even though you follow through calmly and consistently—if she has her own secret stash of identical poker chips. Beware of counterfeiting, particularly if you're busy setting limits with more than one child at a time. If Billy and his sister Sally are each working for poker chips (even if Billy's working toward earning a new CD and Sally is working toward earning new soccer cleats), better to assign green chips to one child and red chips to the other.

And if Grandma or a best friend takes Sally to the mall anyway, why would she bother making her bed?

This can happen by accident, as when Mom forgets to tell her parents that going to the mall is a special treat that must be earned and Grandma, always eager to please, gladly offers to spend the day shopping with her granddaughter. It can happen when co-parents fail to communicate and cooperate. And it can happen intentionally and with malice, as when divorced parents compete for a child's affection and, in the process, undermine not only the other parent's authority but the child's security as well.

When adults compete to win a child's affections, each sabotages the other's opportunity to provide security. The world becomes unpredictable. The child may be celebrating her success—*Yes! I'm going to the mall!*—but her anxiety is needlessly building.

Practical Pointer:

REWARDS MUST BE EARNED; RESOURCES MUST BE FREE

There is a tension between the idea of oiling the wheel that doesn't squeak and the idea of being an emotional anchor. Be careful not to confuse the two.

Your love, affection, and caring are constants, regardless of your child's behavior. These things never have to be earned; they just exist—even when you're mad; even when you're apart.

Some tangible things are simply assumed in the same way. These include food, clothing, and shelter. Basic safety, nutrition, and comforts shouldn't depend upon behavior or need to be earned, at least in childhood. (Unfortunately, many adults struggle every day to ensure that they have these essential, basic resources.)

It's the other stuff that we make contingent in our children's lives. What and how is up to you. In many families, screen time and cell phones, later bedtimes and curfews, use of the car or the bike, spending money and certain privileges must be earned and can be lost. Talking openly about the distinction between resources that are always there and rewards that must be earned can allay many children's fears and improve their successes.

CHAPTER NINE

· · · · · · · · · ·

BOUNDARIES

There is no out
until there's in;
There is no you
until there's me.

Drip. Drip.

A billion repeated experiences spanning a lifetime distinguish "me" from "not me," "mine" from "not mine." Self coalesces like a drip drawn out of the ocean. Some of these billion experiences are universal and elemental and primitive: The newborn's discovery that need and fulfillment are no longer instant and connected. The infant's shock of physical independence that occurs with every separation, and the corresponding joy of reunion and reconnection. Even the let-go emptiness of sleep and the hold-tight awareness of waking to a familiar and safe world.

When a child's earliest experiences of this back-and-forth rhythm are seriously disrupted by illness or trauma, by the inconstancy or emotional absence of caregivers, basic issues of identity and relatedness can be dented or permanently damaged. It's as if a window of opportunity is open during the first few years of life, but if the essential foundation of self isn't poured or is poured poorly during this period, all that comes after may be unstable.

If, however, the child has the benefit of an early foundation—even if it's flawed and imperfect, scarred by loss or change or upset—a healthy self can be constructed. Boundaries can be erected on this foundation like the walls that frame a building, gradually answering and re-answering the questions that refine identity.

Who I am?

What do I think and feel?

Where do I belong?

Am I lovable?

This process is known as internalization: taking within self those structures that once contained you from without. We learn to regulate our own behavior by internalizing limits and consequences. We learn to make sense out of time by internalizing routines and rituals. And we grow an identity by internalizing the boundaries that once held us tight.

Boundaries break vast physical space into comprehensible and meaningful chunks, the way that walls define the rooms within your home. They partition experience into "in" and "out," "self" and "not self." They draw experiences and feelings and relationships into orbit around a coherent center and contain the whole constellation within the emerging idea of "me."

Boundaries can be visible and (literally) concrete, or as abstract and existential as the ideas of personal space, privacy, identity, and confidentiality. They can be as leaky as a sieve or as impenetrable as a steel vault. They can be as rigid and unresponsive as a window nailed shut in its frame, well suited to winter but uncomfortable in August, or as flexible as a sapling, bending to every breeze.

Although the boundaries that define self can become ingrained over time, they are never entirely set in stone. This is bad news for happy, healthy people who are abruptly scarred by trauma, which can dramatically change self and relatedness. The rape victim, for example, whose physical and emotional integrity—the profound sense of boundedness that defines self—is brutalized by an aggressor and, then again, by the legal system that demands public disclosures. Or the survivor of a car wreck who endures amputation, grateful to be alive but resentful and grieving his loss. He is forced to redefine body and self and relationships. "Who am I without an arm?" he wonders. "What does my new dependence on others mean about my identity and value?"

The widowed partner or the bereaved parent, physically whole and untouched by the horror that killed a loved one, is forced to redefine the boundaries and meaning of self no less than the rape victim or the amputee. Having incorporated her husband or son into who she is and how she thinks of herself, she is forced by this loss to suddenly renegotiate identity, personality, and relationships.

The boundaries that define self are tweaked by a hundred tiny interactions every day, and can be shattered by trauma. Loss and grief and rage and guilt. A whole and coherent identity filled with purpose and commitment, optimism and empathy and generosity, can be lost, leaving the victim feeling overwhelmed and confused, oceanic and unbounded, or shuttered, closed, and claustrophobic.

And you and I, sitting comfortably and safe right here, cope with the idea of trauma by imagining that it's distant. We pretend that "it couldn't happen to me." The fact is that even if you are lucky enough to sidestep sexual assault, traumatic injuries, and the death of loved ones, your identity is being eaten away right this minute, as I type and as you read, the way a million tiny piranha devour an elephant. This is the reality of the wonderful-terrible digital age in which we live. Every boundary is blurred. Everything that we might once have called private and personal, or secret and sacred is spilled into the cloud for anyone with the time and the right tools to dissect or distort or simply steal.

But wait. There's good news here as well. The malleable nature of the boundaries that define self also allow change for the better. The closed and claustrophobic self can become open and giving. The rigid and demanding self can become sensitive and responsive. The diffuse, leaky, chameleon-like self can coalesce to become whole.

Powerful positive life experiences can invite a redefinition of self for the better the same way that trauma can demand redefinition for the worse. For some, religion provides that corrective experience. For others, it's exercise. For some it's a twelve-step group. For still others, it's psychotherapy. We know one thing about all of these and similar emotional healing experiences. Putting aside all the fancy words and rituals, as long as a foundation was poured in infancy, all that is necessary for positive change is a single, trusting, constant relationship. An emotional anchor. The feeling of being held tight and let go.

Held tight and let go.

Childhood Boundaries

The existential and intangible thing that we call "self" is shaped in childhood by the most mundane and concrete experiences. The rails of the crib and the edges of the bed; the doors that define rooms; and the walls that distinguish your home from neighboring homes. Each of these and scores of other barriers and dividers of every sort create physical separations between parent and child. Separation is practice at self-containment. Separation is a moment of letting go, sandwiched between moments of feeling held tight.

How and when and how long we create these practice separations is a matter of culture and context and the very specific needs of each parent-child relationship within each family and community. This means that, within the extremes of neglect and abuse, abandonment, and enmeshment, there can be no universal user's manual to raising healthy children.

Should your kids be home-schooled? Should mother and child or the entire clan sleep and bathe together? Should the door on the bathroom be open or closed when you're showering or using the toilet? Should there even be doors on rooms or walls within the home? A practice known as "attachment parenting" teaches that children thrive when the boundaries within family are few or none. But all theories aside, necessity has often required communal living. Clans lived in caves for eons before we invented two-by-fours and wallboard and *Frozen* wallpaper. In truth, many of the separations common to our twenty-first-century, middle-class American culture (including public school) are an artifact of prosperity and successful marketing schemes.

This is not to say that we should sleep and eat and bathe pig-pile like so many Neanderthals or puppies. And this is certainly not to advocate for or against attachment parenting. True, the boundaries that define identity will emerge even among children raised in these relatively unbounded environments, but when practices within the home are starkly different from practices elsewhere in the community, stigma can arise. Taunting and teasing and bullying result—destructive social pressures that function to force outliers to conform—with the side effect of damaging self-esteem.

Community is a container. It holds families the same way that parents hold their children.

What is common across parenting practices, cultures, and generations is the essential experience of holding tight and letting go. No matter whether the newborn is handed over to a wet nurse or allowed to breastfeed with Mom at will through his first six years, separation occurs. What matters is how parent and child mutually manage the emotions that arise and how these choices fit into the encompassing social environment. How anxiety is regulated first between parent and child and later, within each, as they develop the boundaries that define separate selves. Far more important than whether mother and child sleep together or apart, whether the door on the bathroom is double locked or missing entirely, is the child's permission to be separate and his welcome upon return.

Children venture farther and farther away from their parents as they grow. They stretch the anchor rope across a lifelong, repeated, back-and-forth movement toward autonomy. Like Bouncing Baby Billy toddling away from Mom, children separate when the seesaw balance of anxiety and adventure favors adventure. They return when the seesaw balance shifts back.

The physical distance between parent and child is a boundary in and of itself, even though it's invisible and permeable. Sound and sight and some scents travel across the distance from parent to toddler, although the child has forsaken the reassurance of touch and holding in favor of adventure. For this reason, the separation inherent in the toddler's earliest explorations is different from the separations imposed by crib rails and bedroom walls and closed doors. The child can maintain emotional contact across the room, but he has to carry it with him in the form of a transitional object and, later, in the form of emotional security, as separations become farther apart and longer.

Because Baby Billy initiated the separation when he wandered off, Mom is likely to experience anxiety first. It starts as caution. Is the door closed? Is the room safe? Where's Fido? Reassured, she lets Billy go but watches carefully, pride and amazement on one side of the seesaw, caution on the other. Her anxiety ratchets up notch by notch as time passes and distance grows, the way that a balloon fills with air. At some point, caution becomes vigilance, vigilance becomes concern, and concern grows into worry. Worry becomes agitation, and agitation threatens to become panic. At this point the balloon is about to burst. But if Mom is a healthy adult, she is able to regulate her own emotions. Her internal thermostat says that caution and vigilance and even concern are tolerable, but agitation and panic are not. She reads and responds to her own internal emotional cues (very likely in the manner that her parents helped her regulate her experience as a child) and pulls Billy back from the brink.

Billy is startled and angry to be interrupted in the midst of his first long explore, but he's held tight. He's engulfed in a sensory experience that is familiar and comforting. Mom's anxiety caused her heartbeat to thunder and her pulse to race and, reading her body like a book, Billy's body responds in kind. He cries and fusses, but the two synchronized bodies calm. Heartbeats slow. Muscles relax.

Where there were briefly two selves separated by a dozen tiny steps, there is once again one oceanic and undifferentiated identity. A drip rising from the pool and then falling back.

This story is reversed when Mom initiates the separation.

The details hardly matter. Mom sets Bouncing Billy in his crib, says "nap time," plants a kiss on his forehead, and walks away. She straps him into his high-chair for a meal. Dad tucks Billy into his big-boy bed, says "sleep tight!" Grandma drops Billy at day camp with a hug. Mom puts Billy on the school bus and waves good-bye. Uncle Fred drops Billy at his dormitory. One way or another, it's all the same: A caregiver initiates a separation. The child is pushed off along the anchor rope. A boundary separates the child from his anchor across space and time, sometimes in the form of a physical barrier. The child is separate and responsible for managing his own seesaw of anxiety.

When Billy is alone in his crib for the night, his anxiety sparks, threatening to burst into flames of panic. If he has the capacity to self-sooth—if the experience is familiar and he clutches his transitional objects tight and he can anticipate reunion—he'll manage his anxiety. The spark will die to an ember, ever-present but not a threat. If he's unable to self-sooth—if the experience is unfamiliar, if he's taxed by hunger or pain or other anxieties, if reunion is uncertain— that spark will ignite upset and then panic. The flames might grow slowly through whining and fussing and crying and then screaming, or they might burst forth suddenly in a consuming conflagration of full-blown terror.

Every one of us has cringed just beyond the doorway, out of sight, trying to be silent and do what must be done despite the storm of hormones and guilt fueling muscles to go back and rescue the child from the horrors of separation. How could I make him sleep alone? How could I send him off to camp? To school?

Evolution has programmed us to respond Superman-like to the primitive sounds that communicate our children's terror. We know the strength of our desire to protect and keep our children safe—we've all heard and relate to those mythical stories about moms lifting automobiles off their injured children. It's hard to repress that urge, to remind yourself that despite the screams, he's safe. It'll be okay. But you must. Rescuing him now, when he's not in true danger, will only teach him that he doesn't need to learn to cope.

But rescuing him now is easy. He can learn to cope another time. If you go back in and pick him up, he'll settle down. He'll smile and tell you that you're the best parent on earth. Your anxiety will settle along with his. That's a very strong incentive. After all, you had a hard day. The boss yelled at you. The car broke down. You burned the toast. It would be nice to feel held by someone.

This is a trap. If you are needy or depressed or insecure, overwhelmed or exhausted, that kind of love and reassurance can be very, very attractive. It can make you feel effective and needed and loved. But it's not healthy. Our job is to meet our children's needs, not the other way around.

Worse still, if you give in to your selfish needs and go back to rescue him from his own anxiety, you are rewarding his screams. You're teaching him that screaming long and loud enough works; that if the wheel squeaks loud enough, the oil will come. Don't rationalize that you're only giving in this one time because you're tired or the neighbors complained or because you have a big meeting in the morning. All of those reasons may be valid and important. Each may be an excellent reason to tag in a trusted parenting partner (Grandma? a babysitter?) so that you can get your needs met, but Baby Billy doesn't know and doesn't care about any of that. All he knows is what works, and if it works today, he's going to do the same things for weeks to come.

Don't go back. Unless there's real danger, once you've initiated the separation, once you've established the boundary, you must be prepared to tolerate the upset. This is what Richard Ferber taught us about getting kids to sleep in their own beds at night. Billy will never learn how to tolerate his own anxiety if he finds that you can't tolerate it for him and with him. He needs to feel that you are confident as you let him go. He needs to hear that your voice is calm, your heartbeat slow, and your breathing rhythmic. He needs the confidence that you will return later to hold him tight. If you can give him these reassurances, the screaming will pass and he will be better able to manage separation the next time.

FERBERIZE ME!

The Ferber Method or "cry it out" has been around for generations. Ferber popularized it recently by talking about "baby training," which, by the way, is secret code for "parent training."

Ferber advocates pre-sleep rituals to calm and soothe the baby and a regular, predictable bedtime. Structure. The parent is then to leave the room while child is still awake, returning to reassure the distressed baby at progressively longer intervals. Reassurance is verbal and visual, but never tactile. Pick-up would calm the baby, but is also likely to start his distress at separation anew.

In the 2006 revised edition of his book Solve Your Child's Sleep Problems, Ferber notably was much more open to the idea of co-sleeping and adapting solutions to individual child and family needs.

Facilitated Separation

Of course, there is a middle ground between holding tight and letting go completely. Transitional objects help a child to carry around a spare dose of the security that he experiences in your arms, even while apart. Indeed, a bit of creativity and today's incredible technology can be used to extend the security you provide, even to the point of corrupting what we used to think of as healthy boundaries. Maybe even to the point that we have to wonder whether our culture is changing the basic idea of self.

We are now able to manufacture artificial umbilical cords that connect parent and child across great distances. In utero, Billy was never separated from Mom. As a toddler, he maintains contact via sight and sound and smell across space. Still later, he carries a bit of Mom's love hidden in the texture, taste, and smell of a beloved teddy bear, blanket, or binky.

Still later, we drop him off at preschool or summer camp or a playdate, trusting that he can manage his own anxiety in small doses and for brief periods. We are certain that his successes build his confidence, allowing him to bootstrap his way toward becoming independent. But what happens to development when anxiety prompts a cell phone call rather than an opportunity to learn self-soothing? What happens when homesickness can be cured via Skype or Face-Time rather than by crying it out with a camp counselor, a teacher, or a friend's mother?

You can help your child manage his separation anxiety by literally tying one end of a skein of yarn to his belt loop and the other end to yours so that he feels connected. You can teach him that when he tugs on the line, you'll tug back like a nod of reassurance and smile across the distance. You can arm your child with a toy-store walkie-talkie and teach him that when he presses the button to talk, you'll reply. And you can plug the old baby monitor in backwards, transmitting from your bedside to his, so that he falls asleep with the illusion that you're right there, by his side. You can use these and many more creative, high-tech solutions to minimize separation and help him manage his anxiety (and your own), but at what cost? If the goal of letting go is to learn to tolerate feeling bounded and apart, however briefly, and to manage the accompanying anxiety, isn't it best to do just that?

Bounded Body, Bounded Mind

Our bodies leak. They need to be refilled and repaired. We drink and we pee. We eat and we poop. We bleed and our noses run and infections leak pus. It may be impolite to recognize these facts so bluntly, but this is the reality that every child learns very early on. The fact that this realization can be scary highlights the development of boundaries.

By the time Billy's thinking is mature enough to worry about the holes in his body that leak, he has had lots of experience with containers and leaking. The milk jug spills. The balloon bursts. The stuffing erupts out of the seam in Pooh Bear's much-loved fluffy head. It's entirely common for a preschooler to worry that all of his blood will leak out of the boo-boo on his knee, creating for some kids a more-or-less fleeting obsession with bandages. It's just as common for children who must undergo surgery to fear that the surgeon will let all of their insides leak out.

Potty training is often complicated by similar anxieties, giving the idea of holding tight and letting go a new dimension of meaning. It sounds funny, but this is precisely the child's dilemma. Holding tight and letting go of his only and best product, literally a piece of himself, can spark anxiety. Another loss. When stress and relationships and experience converge just so, a child may refuse to let go—holding tight to the point of constipation and impaction, even to the extreme of prompting terrifying and intrusive medical procedures that may be necessary for physical health but which can also confound the foundation of "me" versus "not me."

To some, diapers are just big Band-Aids. They keep the contents of self intact—the stuffing sewn up tight—and the boundaries secure. Giving up diapers or later, transitioning from Pull-Ups to underwear, can bring with it the panic associated with separation. Letting go. Falling from ten thousand feet without a parachute.

And then there's sex. The universal taboo on exposing children to adult physical intimacies and the volumes of laws and ethics that codify this prohibition create a very concrete boundary. Children who are one way or another exposed to adult sex often experience it as an act of violence, complete with screaming. It appears to be an unimaginable breach of boundaries—a complete loss of self.

Unfortunately, it's no longer sufficient to make sure that the doors are closed and the sounds are muffled. We must also create boundaries that protect our children both from the constant flood of media representations of sex that pervade our world and from the predators who seek to undermine those safeguards. All three of these efforts are necessary—protecting our children from our own physical intimacies, from sex in the media, and from predators—but they're not sufficient.

Private Parts

Boundaries define what is in and what is out. What is out is foreign and may be forbidden. What is in coalesces to become identity.

We often use the word "private" to define what is inside the boundary that defines "me" and "mine." We teach our children that it declares what is untouchable and unshareable. We use it to describe our homes (as in "private property") to create an invisible boundary that keeps strangers out. We use it describe a bedroom or an office space or a specific drawer to keep curious others out. We use it to describe what goes on in the bathroom and in the parents' bedroom behind closed doors. And we use the word "private" to define a child's body as his or her own.

Privacy is a reassuring container. It communicates the idea that what is within is held tight. Our society has historically granted most people the right to certain privacies. As parents, we translate these rights for our children by talking about the "bubble" that defines personal space and the sanctity of "private parts."

How Private Is Private?

Is a child's personal privacy a right or a privilege? No one can answer this for you, but it's important to keep one caution in mind as you consider your family's policies: Safety always comes first. You might decide to allow your teenager freedom on the Internet. You might agree that the bathroom door can be shut. You might even allow the kids to put locks on their bedroom doors. You might promise not to read her journal (even though she leaves it out and open on the kitchen table) or not to read his text messages. But you must make it clear that if ever you're concerned for safety, you will open doors and unlock locks and read journals and text messages in whatever way that you feel is necessary. Better to clarify this now than compound a scary time with a needless sense of betrayal.

Other forms of privacy must be earned. They are privileges that come with responsibilities and risks. To draw a boundary prematurely or too rigidly, granting a child privacy inappropriately, can be harmful.

The best example concerns privacy and media access. Is it an intrusion to read your child's emails over his shoulder? To monitor his Tweets and Instagrams, read his text messages, or track his phone (and thus his location) with GPS? Maybe. And maybe they'll rant and rave about the intrusion, but maybe they'll be reassured. And maybe they'll be safer. Giving your children unsupervised and unlimited access to media of any type is like giving them the keys to the candy store. They'll sing your praises all day and then they'll stuff themselves until they're sick.

Giving your child unsupervised media access is akin to what happens if Mom sets Bouncing Baby Billy down without a thought and leaves him to toddle off, unsupervised, while she goes out for a cigarette. Billy needs his anchor present. He needs to feel contained, even if being picked up enrages him. Our children need to know that you're there, monitoring their media access in the same way, ready to reel them back in if they toddle off too far into the World Wide Web. If and when you give them Internet and cell phone and Xbox access, do so with the understanding that you will be looking over their shoulders not because you don't trust them, but because you don't trust everyone else.

On Cynicism, Safety, and Boundaries

Our squeaky wheel, trauma-focused, scared and very scary culture induces a necessary degree of paranoia. Hypervigilance. Our baseline anxiety is jacked up like an athlete on steroids, ever-ready to burst out of the starting blocks, full speed ahead.

Living on red alert is physically and emotionally exhausting. The experience diminishes one kind of neurotransmitter and enhances others, changing brain chemistry. Children raised in red-alert environments like war zones and abusive homes develop a very different sense of self and relatedness to others.

In the months after the horrific events of September 11, 2001, I distinctly remember expecting every airplane overhead to explode. For weeks after the Colorado and Louisiana movie theater shootings, theaters around the country were deserted. How long before we have metal detectors in every public entryway? Today's grade schools conduct practice lockdowns for fear of gun violence much the same way that they hold fire drills. Preschools and pediatrician's offices teach very young children the difference between "good touch" and "bad touch."

This culture-induced and culture-endorsed state of red alert wariness was never as clear to me as it was in this incident: Smiling and skipping, five-year-old Sally greeted Mom at home after a weekend with Dad. Mom asked about the weekend and heard Sally reply, "Daddy taught me all about sex."

If you agree that Mom's instant panic was warranted, you've proven the point. We are on red alert, anxiety waiting to burst forth at any moment for any reason, confirming our worst fears.

Mom called her lawyer and child protective services and the pediatrician. After many tearful weeks, several intrusive examinations, and thousands of dollars in attorney's fees, a child advocate calmly and carefully interviewed Sally about the time she spends with each of her parents. Smiling but confused and missing her daddy, Sally talked about how he'd taught her all about "sex."

Spiders and butterflies and ants and bumblebees.

"'Sects," the little girls repeated as if speaking to a deaf person.

"Insects."

When we're anxious, we see threats everywhere we look so we hold our children tighter and longer. We let them go less often and less far and with much greater anxiety. We create boundaries and borders and walls that are harder to breach. We define self and defend against others more quickly and more harshly. We do so in the interest of safety, but again we need to ask: At what cost?

Practical Pointer:

HOLDING TIGHT, HOLDING TIGHTER

Running alongside your daughter as she pedals her two-wheeler for the first time, you don't need to let go. You could hold tight endlessly, stop her when you're out of breath. Keep her home and safe in her bed, except that doing so would be almost as harmful as the dangers you fear.

How much risk should you take? Where does caution become over-protection and caring become making you a helicopter parent?

No one can answer these questions for you. In many instances, the child's own push to be let go will gradually erode how long and how hard you hold her tight. In other instances, books like this, expert opinions, and community practices will matter; they will help you determine what's right for your family.

The hardest situation is how you let go after a serious loss. We all lose perspective in this situation. You let her go yesterday and she was injured, so how can you let her go today? You faced trauma in a similar situation yourself, so how can you protect her now?

This is a balancing act that no one should try to manage alone. Let your co-parent, your friends, and trusted professionals guide you. Keep your fingers on the pulse of your own anxiety and be careful! Your fears and worries are catchy. Do you want her to fear something just because you do?

· · · · · · · · · ·

CHAPTER TEN

ROUTINES AND RITUALS

Life, like naptime,
is easier to manage
when you understand that
all things have a beginning,
a middle,
and an end.

Our brains are first and foremost difference detectors. We reflexively distinguish known from unknown, familiar from unfamiliar, so that we can devote our finite energies to that which is new. Were it not for our capacity to detect differences, every moment of every day would be overwhelming. In a world in which everything is new and equally deserving of attention, our senses would be swamped, resulting first in panic and then in total breakdown.

The structures that parents impose on children (and society imposes on us all) diminish anxiety by reducing novelty. Avoiding overload. Limits and consequences reduce an infinite number of possible behaviors to those that will be rewarded and those that will be punished. Boundaries reduce the infinity of physical space into "me" and "not me," and in the process define identity. Routines and rituals break the intangible, invisible expanse of time into a domino-like succession of predictable events.

A-then-B-then-C.

Long before clocks, we relied on nature to make sense out of the passage of time. Cycles of light and dark defined days. Cycles of cold and hot defined seasons. The shifting appearance of the moon from new to full and back again defined months.

In the same way that children internalize the structures that parents provide, species internalize the structures that nature provide. Our bodies' sleep-wake rhythm is synchronized to the planet's day-night cycle. Our energy and neurotransmitters and hormones shift with the season. Menstrual cycles correspond to the lunar calendar and, in a final *ta-da!* nod to nature's wisdom, the menstrual cycles of women who live together will often spontaneously fall in sync one with another.

Our children are acclimated to these rhythms long before they are born. Shifts in Mom's heart rate and body temperature, activity level and two specific hormones—cortisol and melatonin—are so successfully communicated to the fetus throughout development that, by ten weeks before delivery, the two have synchronous REM sleep cycles.

Understanding how completely mom's body regulates her child's experience gives the idea of holding tight and letting go a new depth of meaning. The miraculous and traumatic letting go that is birth is far more than the loss of immediate gratification. It means the loss of regulation as well. Gone are the signals that make sense out of time. The predictable drumbeat rhythm that always before set the pace and sequence of experience is suddenly absent.

I imagine that the newborn feels at birth like Dorothy did in her dream on her way to Oz, clutching her bed as it tumbled through terrifying visions moving randomly at her and away, crosswise and up and down, across the clouds. Or, more exactly, perhaps the newborn feels like a damp sock in the drier: Without identity or order or direction. Out of control and overwhelmed. But at least the sock, if it had awareness, might take some comfort in knowing that it's contained in a steel drum. Its experience is somehow contained. The chaos can only go so far.

The newborn doesn't have even that faint reassurance until he is first held tight. He is flailing, falling without a parachute. Every sense on overload. Panicked. Until suddenly he's not. He's contained and with that containment, rhythm reappears. Different, but the same. Her scent. Her sounds. Calm returns like the drier reaching the end of its cycle, the contents settling in a heap. Like Dorothy touching down amidst Technicolor flowers. There is no sense of next. Only now. And now. And now again.

Held tight in the now, chest to chest with Mom, heartbeats find synchrony anew. Breathing slows. Brainwaves and hormone levels fall into a familiar and comforting cadence. Briefly wrenched apart from his mother, the child was incomplete—unbounded, uncontained; drowning in unfamiliar, screaming anxiety—and is once again whole. Anchored. Bounded. Familiar. Calmed.

And then he's let go. He has no sense of how long comfort existed or if it will return. To you and me, it's only a momentary respite. You need to use the bathroom. The doctor needs to perform a quick exam. Even apart, you still have one tear-filled, tired eye always on the brand-new baby—"I can't believe I made him. He's so beautiful!"—but he doesn't know that. You're completely confident that the separation will end. Experience has taught you the domino-like succession of time, so you can briefly fight back the powerful urge to hold him. You can talk yourself through the anxiety. Hug your partner, talk to the doctor. Take your medicine. Nod politely like you're actually listening.

The nurse is taking care of Billy. It'll just be a minute. She'll bring him right back.

But Billy knows none of this. He can't anticipate reunion. In the present now, chaos has resumed. All Billy has is now. And now. And now. It's not even fair to write about "another" or "the next" now, or to suggest that this now is different from the now that just passed. These words would suggest that Billy is able to connect "now" with something that came before or something that is yet to come. He can't. There is only held tight or let go. Calm and chaos without sequence or sense.

91

Held tight means order.

Let go means chaos.

Until the two become connected. Until the difference detector in his head recognizes this first, most primitive, and important sequence: Hold-tight leads to let-go leads to hold-tight. Separation leads to re-union. Anxiety can be tolerated. It will end.

This *now* leads to the next *now*.

Experiences are strung together like beads on a necklace—like dominoes in line—making it suddenly possible to anticipate the next bead, one at a time. Chaos is a little more manageable if calm is next along the string of experience. Anxiety is a little less overwhelming if reassurance follows.

Letting go is tolerable if it reliably leads to holding tight.

The baby's capacity to expect or predict or anticipate—to infer next from last—may be only from one bead on the string to the bead that follows, but even that requires the idea of linearity. There is a string. There can be order. This is a huge leap forward from living in random tumult and chaos.

The idea that events occur in sequence opens the door to self-soothing. Once the child becomes able to expect calm and comfort, managing pain is a bit easier. Anxiety is reduced. Hormones settle. Blood that floods the body to enable fight or flight is redirected to the brain to enable more difference detection—learning.

Body rhythms once familiar in utero are re-established in those first joyful-painful-endless days after you bring the baby home. New parents eat and sleep and bathe helter-skelter around the baby's needs. We pick him up and put him down, clean him and diaper him, feed him and rock him almost at random, trying to learn his signals as he tries to learn ours. Our difference detectors are running full tilt, trying to make sense out of experience. This is the most immersive language learning lesson anyone will ever endure, but the language learned has no words. It's a language of sequence or order, more like music than lexicon, because it relies on rhythm.

In those first days and weeks after birth, parent and child (re-) establish mutual rhythm. An A-then-B-then-C pattern of need and comfort, need and comfort. This is likely as poor a substitute for the rhythm that spontaneously and unconsciously arose in utero as it is a poor approximation of the rhythms of the adult world, but it works for a while. It likely begins with many cycles of food and rest and elimination as mother and child (re-)build their strength. Gradually, the rhythm slows. The cycle lengthens. The pattern between parent and child more or less synchronizes with the pattern between parent-child and family, and then between family and community, community and nature.

A-then-B-then-C becomes more than a cycle of wakefulness and comfort; it becomes a way of thinking-feeling. It's not that the baby hears the front door open and says to himself, "Mom's home. Food's coming." It's the sensory-emotional association between cause and effect. Door sound anticipates comfort.

Let-go anticipates hold-tight.

Scream and flail anticipates pick-up. Pick-up anticipates calm.

Supper anticipates warm, soothing bath, which anticipates sleep.

Alarm clock anticipates breakfast, which anticipates school bus, which anticipates friends.

Work anticipates paycheck, which anticipates buying, which anticipates pleasure (or, in the case of bills, pain relief).

When the world is in chaos, there is no room left for novelty, learning, and growth. Exploration shuts down. We retreat into the familiar. But when the world is ordered and predictable, anxiety is diminished. The difference detector can devote greater resources to novelty and growth. This reality often prompts me to recommend to parents that their goal should be to be boring.

Boring means predictable. It means that the world is familiar and safe. If little or no emotional energy needs to be devoted to coping with home, then most or all of that energy can be directed outward. Go ahead and have fun. Laugh and play and dance, but make sure that events like bedtime and mealtime and bath time and homework—who is there and when—are all familiar. That life at home is A-then-B-then-C.

BOREDOM, ADHD, AND AUTISTIC DISORDERS

Attention deficit hyperactivity disorder (ADHD) and autism spectrum disorders (ASD) pose special challenges that can affect every aspect of a child's life, parenting, and the family's well-being.

In one conception, people with ADHD are starved for stimulation. They constantly need new and active input to keep their brains satisfied. They are bored quickly and easily and often, but not in a reassured and calmed way. Instead, when these people become bored, they may become fidgety, disruptive, or even dangerous.

People with ASD (Asperger's syndrome, for example) can have the opposite problem. The world (particularly the social and emotional world) can feel so stimulating that they are constantly on overload. They need holding tight and structure to reduce stimulation, not to the point of boredom but low enough so they are able to function.

Only a qualified health care professional can help you make these diagnoses and recommend how best to modify your parenting practices to meet the child's needs.

Creating Routines

One of the most important things we can do as parents is also one of the easiest. We can create routines in our children's lives. We can purposefully decide that bedtime will be the same A-then-B-then-C pattern every day. That wake-up will be the same X-then-Y-then-Z pattern every day.

Mealtime predictably means set the table, turn off screens, eat what you're served, clear your dishes.

Homework time is always the same: get off the bus; eat a healthy snack at the counter; clean up the dishes; do math, French, and science at the kitchen table; review with Mom; go out to play.

Wake-up schedule is consistent: hear the alarm ring; use the bathroom and get dressed; eat breakfast at the table; pack backpacks; get shoes, coat, and hat; catch the bus.

Every day is wake-up, school, homework time, supper time, bedtime. Every week follows the same schedule Monday, Tuesday, Wednesday, Thursday, Friday, Saturday, and Sunday. Every month contains weeks, and every year contains months, and the seasons shift in order, and every birthday and every holiday are each A-then-B-then-C—routines within routines within routines. When time is ordered and events are predictable, anxiety is quelled. Security and confidence are fueled.

Of course, raising a child in absolute and complete order would probably cripple his ability to cope with change. We need practice managing accidents and flat tires and emergencies as well because they happen. A child who has never known chaos could hardly be expected to cope when it finally occurs. This would be a strong argument against the value of perfect routine, if it were possible. As it is, complete and utter routine is barely even conceivable.

Life happens. Burned toast and snowstorms and exploding diapers and broken ankles and injuries and death are all inescapable. Go ahead and do your best to make your child's world boring. A-then-B-then-C. None of us can ever succeed completely, but the success you do achieve will help ensure that the resources are there when crises arise.

Bedtime, Letting Go, and Routines

Exhausted and aggravated parents complain so often about getting Billy to sleep at night that the topic deserves a discussion all its own.

I think this subject comes up more often than others—getting Billy up in the morning or on the school bus each day—because the battle is fought when everyone is at their worst. Exhausted at day's end, we all regress to earlier, less mature, and less successful ways of functioning. Ten-tear-old Billy starts acting more like a needy five-year-old. Mom and Dad give up their practiced, calm and reassuring voices in favor of loud and angry demands. All of this stokes the anxiety associated with letting go, which is a necessary part of bedtime.

Going to sleep, after all, means letting go not only of anchors and routines and familiarity, but also of awareness. It's a loss of complete control. It's no surprise that generations of churchgoing children buffered themselves against their fear of oblivion by reciting, "Now I lay me down to sleep, I pray the Lord my soul to keep, and if I die before I wake, I pray the Lord my soul to take." The surprise, in fact, is that these children slept at all.

No matter your religious affiliation, practices, and beliefs, we can help our children manage their anxiety about letting go at bedtime by making the process routine. A-then-B-then-C. But beware of one particular trap:

After supper, Dad does the dishes while Mom reads the newspaper and Billy kills aliens, steals race cars, or builds cubical people in cubical worlds (or maybe even does something that doesn't require a screen). If bedtime is nine o'clock, Mom interrupts the fun at eight thirty to announce that it's time for Billy to take his bath, brush his teeth, put on his pajamas, and then go to bed. War ensues. Tempers flare. The natural anxiety of bedtime is compounded by the unnecessary anxiety of conflict.

This routine is backwards. Why would Billy comply?

The Premack principle teaches that if two things must get done, it's best to tackle the least enjoyable first. Accomplishing that task then earns the natural reward of the second, more enjoyable activity.

Billy has no incentive to stop playing and get ready for bed. Playing is much more enjoyable. Better would be a routine that calls for all get-ready-for-bed activities to be accomplished before playtime begins. That way, Billy is motivated to bathe and brush and dress in order to have more time shooting bad guys online. Less fuss = more compliance. Later, the transition from play into bed will be far less challenging.

Many parents concede the bedtime battle by agreeing to lay down with the child while he falls asleep or even to invite the child to sleep in the parents' bed. Whether either makes sense to you will be a matter of culture, ethics, and personal beliefs, but if you give in, beware: Once Billy's bedtime A-then-B-then-C routine includes laying down with Mom, turning the lights out, and then falling asleep, it will be very hard to change. Transitional objects and creative technologies may help, but nothing will be as powerfully reassuring as Mom herself.

School Resistance and Refusal

The same ideas apply to the morning routine. Make access to the TV, the computer, and the cell phone all contingent on first getting dressed, eating breakfast, and packing up the backpack. If the devices come out first, every school day will be a battle.

But even when the routine minimizes anxiety, getting on the bus or getting out of the car in the car pool line can be another excruciating demand to let go—to separate from the anchor. Rage and tears result. Embarrassment blossoms. Parents feel inadequate in their peers' and in teachers' eyes, but it's a battle that must be fought and won every time. Giving in even once—rewarding Billy's school refusal by letting him stay home—will make the battle ten trillion times louder and longer and more painful tomorrow.

As with the bedtime battle, transitional objects can help. A piece of the emotional security held tight in his hand, carried in his pocket, stuffed in his backpack, worn on his wrist or around his neck. A note tucked in his lunchbox. A photo taped in his locker. A trinket delivered to the teacher the day before to be received upon timely arrival the next morning. In some instances, arranging a midday call or video chat is enough to refuel and reassure, but these solutions come with a familiar warning: If the goal is to manage the separation, interim contact with you can become a crutch.

Faculty and staff may be able to help when school refusal is intense and severe. A teacher may be willing to invite Billy to arrive early to be her special helper before the other children arrive. A counselor may be available to escort Billy from the car directly to her office for some quiet time. The school nurse or principal or a beloved gym teacher might be available to spend ten minutes midday or as needed or, often best, as a reward for getting to class on time. In each of these cases, Billy is being offered a new emotional anchor within the school. Not a substitute for you, but a spare can of fuel to help him manage until he gets home to you.

There's one further clue there, in that last sentence. In the same way that Billy anticipated the comfort of your arms when he was still just a bouncing baby, now that he's older he needs to be able to anticipate the reassurance of your presence when he gets off the school bus at the end of the day. He's been off on a long explore—okay, so it was only six hours, but it's been emotionally taxing. His tank is nearly empty. How can you be there to refuel him?

If you are physically present to greet him after school, make sure that you're also emotionally present. If he climbs in the car or gets off the bus or walks in the door only to find you busy and distracted, his needs go unmet and he will find a way to get them filled. He may squeak loud and long enough until he finally gets your attention, or he may simply be unable to manage homework or chores or his annoying little sister until he's refueled. One way or another, depending on his age, personality, and circumstances, he must be held tight.

Put away the laptop, cell phone, and spreadsheets. Can you commit ten or fifteen uninterrupted minutes to your kids at the end of their school day? Can you join them in their world, ask about their day without pressure or interrogation? Can you share a snack, take a walk, have a cuddle, listen to a song, or play a game?

And if you can't be physically present? You can still offer the same kind of emotional presence from a distance. Can you call or video-chat when Billy gets home? Perhaps you can leave a special note on the kitchen counter every afternoon that says something more than "do your homework." Or, take one more turn in your long-standing one-move-a-day game of checkers or Scrabble so that when he goes back to the board and sees your move, he reconnects to the ongoing thread of the game and the continuity of your love.

CONNECTING WITH KIDS

Many parents struggle with how to connect with their children without interrogating. This is particularly difficult when the child is a teenager and supersensitive to privacy and when parents live apart, trying to respect the boundary between the two homes.

"How are you?" and "How was your day?" and "What's up?" are excellent ways to begin if all you want is a grunt. These questions are too vague. Even among mature adults, they usually elicit only rote social niceties like "Fine, thanks. How're you?"

In some cases, you're better off following up on a specific thread of conversation. Yesterday, Billy mentioned auditioning for the school play. Today, you ask if he's heard about roles. Last week you helped him on his Portugal project, so today you can follow up. But don't ask only about grades. Ask how he felt about it, what the other kids said, and how the other kids' projects went as well.

In other cases, you can help by structuring the answer for him. Instead of, "What happened today?" ask him what he did today that he's proud of or ask, "What happened today that made you mad? Sad? Scared? Happy?"

Practical Pointer:
WHEN ROUTINES BECOME COMPULSIONS

Some people cope with overwhelming anxiety by developing routines and rituals that are completely unchangeable and sometimes even irrational. In the extreme, a rigid routine is called a compulsion. With or without circular thoughts, compulsions can be evidence of obsessive-compulsive disorder or OCD.

OCD is a relatively common psychiatric disorder. An individual with OCD might find that specific worries or fears go round and round his thinking endlessly and painfully until he performs a certain action that gets him out of the loop. Fears about germs and contamination, illness, loss and death often fuel the obsessive thinking. The associated ritual may be an exaggeration of a common behavior, like hand washing, or might be completely unique to the individual, like touching each elbow with the opposite pinky finger three times in rapid succession.

Like the rituals that healthy parents create to anchor their kids, the OCD sufferer's rituals diminish anxiety, but the extremes of obsession and compulsion get in the way of living. A parent with OCD may be limited in his ability to read and respond to a child's needs. A child with OCD may not be able to manage friendships or learning like her peers.

OCD must be diagnosed and treated by a skilled mental health professional. Anti-anxiety medications and cognitive behavioral therapies are often helpful.

. . . .

CHAPTER ELEVEN

MPG: HOW MANY MILES DO YOU GET TO EACH HUG?

I carry one bottle of your love with me.
I drink from it constantly,
yet somehow it is always full.

The fetus is held tight in the womb. He exists without time or limits; oceanic. Need and fulfillment are immediate and connected. He cannot know that he is held tight because he has never yet been let go.

Birth is letting go. It means the discovery of unfulfilled need and frustration. In the gap between need and need fulfillment, the first seeds of self are planted. We mature in the painful-exciting-terrifying absence of holding tight, learning that we are bounded and needy. Learning how to feel emotionally anchored, how to manage anxiety, and what lies beyond the safety of Mom's arms. We learn to trust and who is trustworthy. We learn to carry security in the palm of our tiny hands a few steps and then a few miles and then a few days away from our anchors. Teddy bears and pacifiers, photographs and lockets, walkie-talkies and video chats buttress the fragile and emerging, encapsulated self.

During childhood and adolescence, we discover anchors farther and farther from home. Teachers and coaches, cliques and gangs, clubs and teams help to hold us tight, however briefly; however imperfectly. They bridge the growing gap between venturing out and returning to Mom's arms—returning to the anchoring familiarity of home—and reinforce the walls of the tentative, young self.

And here we are in youth, blinded by a bright, shiny new identity.

Imagine Billy with his first car. He's nineteen or twenty years old. He washes it and polishes it reverently. He revs the engine at every stoplight just for the attention, unaware and uncaring that what he gets back is largely embarrassment and disdain. The vehicle is ten years old and dented and scratched. It needs a paint job. It coughs and sputters and spews black exhaust, but it goes, it's his, and he'll brag about it to all who will listen.

The analogy is apt. If holding tight means getting emotionally refueled, then we can talk about where and how Billy gets gas and how far a fill-up will take him—his miles per gallon or mpg. Back when he was still a bouncing baby, he had to borrow Mommy's "car." A loaner. It had a tiny tank that needed to be filled often, but he had the highest quality fuel that he'll ever find. Topped off, he'd zoom across the living room floor, barefoot and pigeon-toed, until either the tank ran dry or Mom would hear a telltale backfire and call him in for a refill.

As he grew, his gas tank's capacity grew too. He could hold more fuel and go farther, but the outings always ended the same way. Scared by the monsters under the bed, indignant about a knee scraped on the playground, or furious about a fight with his new best friend, he'd always end up running on empty, needing a tow; or near-empty and recalled for repairs just in time. Either way, Mom was there, the fuel was rich, and the station was always open.

Daycare and preschool, kindergarten and grade school, summer camp and sleepovers taught Billy to carry a spare can of gas in his trunk. Just a gallon or two. Just in case. This meant that five- and seven- and nine-year-old Billy could go farther with greater confidence. The tank ran dry less often and, when it did, he could refill it partially by himself. His need for pit stops and tow trucks became less frequent. Of course, there was the occasional fender bender and the couple of times that he got totaled, but that's the nice thing about metaphoric automobiles. No real damage was done. A lesson was learned. Mom or Dad held him tight for a couple of hours or a couple of days; once for a whole week when he fell off the seesaw and broke his arm. Refueling. Banging out the dents and repairing the scratches. Upgrading the tank. Then he was off again.

At ten or twelve or fifteen, Billy realized that there are other gas stations out there. Opportunities to top off the tank a little or a lot, even to refill the spare can he always carries, just in case. The fuel might not be as rich. The octane lower. His mpg decreased. But these other stations were new and exciting. They held him tight briefly, then let him go, and it felt good.

Now Billy is twenty. Somehow, without ceremony or transfer of title, the car he once borrowed from Mom has become his own. He zips around his ever-expanding world fearlessly—too fearlessly, some would say—getting refilled at work and in class, on the basketball court and just hanging out with his friends. He stops home long enough to empty the refrigerator, annoy his little sister, and leave wet towels on the bathroom floor. He would never admit (and may not even realize) that the unchanged familiarity of his childhood bedroom, Mom's and Dad's fleeting hug and kiss, a family meal or the occasional holiday get-together all refuel and rebuild him unlike any other relationship he has ever known.

So far.

Sure, he's dated. His few girlfriends were glad to go out for a drive, to burn a gallon or two of gas without ever fulfilling some vague and unstated promise that hung in the air between them. Sure, one or two have polished his bumpers. One even took a look under the hood. But none has yet refueled him. Dating was like a fun ride with the top down and the music blaring, but he always returned to the dorm or the apartment or back home, to Mom and Dad, in need of a fill-up.

And then along came Honey.

By some magical convergence of need and opportunity, mothers' meddling, fate and faith and chance, hormones and development,

Billy and Honey met. Taking her for a ride accomplished something impossible—a miracle of the physics of emotion. His tank was more full after they were together than before. Soon enough they realized that the act of filling the other's tank replenished their own.

We call this love, but in so doing we create a problem.

The emotional fuel that Billy's mom has provided since before he was born, and will continue to offer far into the future, is also called love. This is the fuel that she infused in him by holding him tight, heartbeat to heartbeat; that she transmitted across the room as he toddled off; that she stuffed back inside the seams of his favorite teddy bear; that she packed up in a note in his lunch box; that she imbued in every birthday card and holiday gift. This is the fuel that she always has close at hand, just in case.

It may be that the problem is an artifact of the English language, but I don't think so. I've never yet discovered a language that has words to distinguish the one-way emotional fuel that parents provide their children from the two-way emotional fuel that adults provide one another. This is the difference between parent-child love and intimate adult-adult love. Using the same word for the two seems to equate things that are very distinct.

Parents refuel children.

Adults refuel one another.

Don't be fooled by the fact that the emotional reciprocity between adults is often out of sync. It must be. Partners take turns giving and taking. Today, Honey is emotionally drained so Billy holds her tight. Tomorrow or next week when Billy is at his limit, overwhelmed, his tank nearly empty, Honey will refill him. They wake up each day and let one another go, confident in their love that if either crashes and burns, the other will be there to tow them in, fill them up, and hold them tight. In this way, each anchors and refuels the other.

But what happens when both tanks are empty at the same time? When even the spare cans carried in the trunk are bone dry? This is the dilemma at the root of many adult relationship conflicts. One or both partners expect to be refueled but both come up empty. The argument might sound like it's about sex (his complaint) or intimacy (her complaint). About cleaning the house or paying the bills, or about an affair. It might sound like it's about money or addiction or violence. In truth, all of these things may be real and deserving of careful attention. But if you hear that the vehicle has stopped working, your first move should be the same as any good mechanic's: check whether the tank is full; examine how and where it gets filled.

HARMFUL ANCHORS

The need to feel anchored is so strong that many victims of abuse and neglect remain in the hurtful environment because it's familiar. The threat of change seems scarier than the familiarity of the harm. The solution is to give the victim a new and safe anchor outside the harmful environment.

It is a sad and painful reality that some people are forced to leave one anchor without having another one waiting. A partner's or parent's death, poverty, a house fire. Eviction, run-away, or rejection. These people are at extremely high risk for many social and physical health ills. Homelessness and indigence, substance dependence and human trafficking.

Our society provides a degree of respite to some people for a set period, and sometimes it's enough. Welfare and housing and food stamps and WIC, for example. Many, however, fall between the cracks—unaware of the anchors that the community can provide, untrusting, or unable to muster the basic skills necessary to acquire them.

It Takes a Village

Most of us let go of one anchor only when we're confident that there's another waiting, ready and available to hold us tight; to refuel us. As children, we need to see our parents in this way—invulnerable and immortal and constant—until we're mature enough to realize that they're not.

As adults, we know that the people upon whom we rely are as human and needy and vulnerable as we are, but that idea is slippery and easily misplaced. We are inclined, instead, to imbue our adult partners with the same super-human qualities we once wished upon our parents, and then resent them for the limits of their very human strength.

As much as any parent or partner might wish to be Superman, always ready to fly to the rescue, always able to save the day, we're all limited and flawed. We all have weaknesses and get sick and injured and eventually die. Accepting this truth, a mature parent does everything for her child that she can, but never alone. She knows that it takes a village to raise a child.

When Bouncing Baby Billy toddled off and found himself overwhelmed, his mom was there, ready to refuel him. But Dad was on standby in the next room, reading the paper. Grandma was napping down the hall, but always with the door open, just in case the young parents wanted help. And when Billy was born, Uncle Phil offered to fly down to help out any time that he was needed.

It takes a village to sustain an adult relationship as well.

To look to your partner to meet all of your needs is more than naïve; it's self-destructive. Expecting him or her to be as invulnerable and ever-present as Superman—as reliable and responsive and attentive as the mother you had, or the mother you wish you'd had—is both a compliment and a catastrophe.

The same is true of any adult who presents himself or herself as the solution to a partner's every need, who perhaps even demands total devotion or total isolation. It is narcissistic and delusional to believe yourself able to fulfill another person's every need, and no less pathological to believe that of another. There is a brittleness in the personality of anyone so incapable of sharing and so unwilling to trust.

With or without an intimate partner, we all need many simultaneous supports. Many anchors. A village to hold us tight. Friends and family and colleagues and neighbors. Faith institutions and the guys at the gym and the book group. We need the Wednesday evening "Hi, how are you? Fine, thanks" banter, the neighborhood barbeques, and even the camaraderie among digital avatars storming a medieval castle. These may be intellectually empty exchanges or profound and insightful dialogues, but either way, they are emotional constants—

anchors—that help to refuel you and hold you tight.

With the benefit of these many connections—threads in a safety net—partners return after a separation a little less needy. A little less demanding. A little better prepared to read and respond to the other's needs. A little better prepared, in fact, when a tiny third person enters the mix.

Practical Pointer:

DON'T FORGET TO ROTATE THE TIRES AND CHANGE THE OIL

If it's not regularly maintained, a car's miles per gallon will diminish over time. The same is true of our children. Your son might have managed a week away at the school's science camp last month but he has a hard time managing a sleepover at a friend's house this week. The change probably doesn't mean a problem, but it may be time for a maintenance check:

1. What other stresses is he managing? Is his schoolwork overwhelming? Is he worried about making the football team or being cast in the play? Has there been new conflict at home? Is Dad away on business? Is Mom sick? Did a new sibling just arrive? Even something as seemingly benign as having company or painting the house can add stress and diminish his mpg.

2. How's his physical health? If he's having trouble sleeping, if his appetite is off, if he's struggling with allergies or an injury or a persistent pain, he may feel less secure and confident away from his anchors.

3. Even if he's fine, he may be less willing or able to let go if someone else is stressed or ill. His mpg will drop dramatically if he fears that you might not be there when he gets home; if he worries that there might be violence or drinking or drugging while he's gone. Does he worry that his sister might get sick or his puppy will die if he's away? Or on the flip side of that coin, does he think he'll miss out on something fun? Exciting news or a party or a present?

CHAPTER TWELVE

REFILLING THE FUEL PUMPS

The physics of things
demands that pouring from one cup into another
empties the first and fills the second.
The physics of relationships
allows that pouring from one cup into another
fills both.

Only evolution's cruel genius would make the ultimate act of holding tight and the ultimate act of letting go one and the same. Sex brings couples together. It is both holding and release. Union and oceanic dissolution. It makes one out of two, and then it makes three. This is brilliant and manipulative all at once because—you've got to wonder—if intercourse and procreation were not connected, would our species still exist? And so it is that, with or without intention, with a modicum of good (or bad) timing, and with the right mix of hormones, adults who turn to one another to be held tight often become parents.

Beware that the noun and the verb are quite distinct. Sex can make you "a parent" (noun), but neither conception nor gestation nor delivery is enough to make you "parent" (verb). "To parent" is to give without expectation of return. To commit yourself to serving as another human being's emotional anchor and thermostat and gas pump. Chauffeur and waitress, nurse and audience, playmate, tutor and taskmaster.

Some come to parenting in the natural course of things. Others go to great lengths to achieve the same goal. Aids and surrogates, medications and interventions, lawyers and fees and insurance dollars. The adult who parents as a result of a spontaneous biological process may have a head start over the adult who raises a child born of her egg carried in another woman's womb, or the adult who adopts at birth or at ten days or at ten months or at ten years. No matter how you get there, the process is the same.

Parenting is the experience, repeated *ad infinitum,* of holding tight and letting go.

If the child has an initial foundation of security in his first couple of years somewhere, with someone, those early biological head starts may mean little over time. What matters to the child's emerging identity is the security of feeling anchored. Held. Contained. The confidence that he can let go, toddle across the room or down the hall or off to college, and come back to be refueled. We are our children's fuel pumps at least as much as we are their anchors. We let them go, their tanks topped off, and then we retrieve them, dented and scraped and empty, and fill them up again.

Many parents give to their children selflessly and eagerly, but not endlessly. It can't be done. There is a bottom to every barrel. Of course, the glue-and-glitter holiday cards, early morning cuddles, and bedtime hugs feel good. His smile of pride and report card successes and even his needy, clinging cries make you feel needed. This is certainly love, pure and simple, but it must not be your fuel. To depend upon your immature child to fill your tank—to anchor and hold and contain you—is a destructive reversal of roles.

The best solution is when parenting can be made into a team sport. A collaboration with an adult partner. A lover or spouse. A roommate or your own parent. Gender and generation and the legal standing of the adult relationship don't matter to the child (even if they may matter to the IRS and the health insurance company). What does matter is the quality of the cooperation, communication, and consistency between parenting partners. This is co-parenting.

Healthy co-parents anchor and refuel one another so that, together, they are better able to anchor and refuel their child. In the healthiest families, co-parents work out ways to tag a partner in when exhaustion builds and when frustration threatens. They self-consciously weave a safety net beneath the child, advising that, "I'll talk to your other parent and we'll let you know." They offer one another perspective and alternatives off-line, away from little ears: "Here's what I think . . ." and "What if we try this next time . . . ?" They share in the joys and the sorrows, the pride and the pain.

They refuel one another so that each is better able to refuel the child.

"I" VERSUS "WE"

Pronouns can be very important.

When a parent responds to a child's need in the first person, using "I," a subtle barrier is built that excludes other people. This is very important when an apology is necessary, as in "I'm sorry that I made a mistake," but it can be destructive as well.

"I decided that you can go" or "I thought about it and you can have a cell phone" excludes co-parents. It makes the speaker a good guy and risks casting the other parent as the bad guy.

Better to use the third person "we" in these situations to knit the child's safety net together tighter.

Not only does healthy co-parenting serve the adults' needs; it works to the child's benefit as well. Feeling connected to more than one anchor—held tight by more than one parent—strengthens feelings of security. When co-parents do their job right, the structures that the child internalizes—limits and boundaries and routines—are that much sounder and clearer and reassuring.

Some adults parent alone, of course. Whether by choice or by chance. Widowed or deserted or untrusting, isolated or anxious and apart. Single parents have only their own very finite emotional fuel to give their child. For those who found that past partners took more than they gave, single parenting may feel like a relief. Like a leak in the gas tank has been repaired, leaving that much more available for the person who needs and deserves the fuel: the child.

For those who have lost a valued parenting partner abruptly, parenting alone can be overwhelming. Grief in all of its torturous and shifting forms—rage and sadness, guilt and neediness—can drain your emotions, depriving a child who has already lost one anchor of a second.

Worse still is the risk to the child whose parents have made parenting into a competitive sport—a contest to win his love, to prove that one parent is better by demonstrating that the other is worse. The single parent's grief and the injured parent's pain and the addicted parent's obsession are each enough to drain emotional resources, leaving a child to feel empty and unanchored. But this parent, engaged in a war in which the child is the prize, is actively and needlessly doing harm. This parent is devoting emotional energy that the child needs and deserves to the selfish and pointless task of proving oneself by decimating someone else, heedless of the fact that that enemy is, in fact, the child's other anchor.

"In Case of a Loss of Cabin Pressure . . ."

Flight attendants remind us routinely: Take care of yourself first. This is not selfishness. It's survival. The parent who takes care of herself first is better able to take care of her child. If you aren't convinced by the airlines' logic, look in the mirror. Do you see your own parent(s) staring back?

Your children are watching. They are destined to do what you do, long before they do what you say. If you want them to be able to take care of themselves someday, to be able to trust others to anchor and refuel and hold them tight, they need permission through your example today.

If you give endlessly to your children with no consideration of your own needs, one of two things is likely to occur. You will either discover that your kids have grown up to become martyrs or they have grown up to become narcissists: painfully refueling others to their own detriment, or constantly demanding that others refuel them. The martyr has built an identity that is self-effacing, his boundaries sieve-like, feeling that he can only be valued for what he gives. The narcissist has built an identity that can never be adequately fulfilled, his boundaries fortress-like and impenetrable.

Neither is happy.

Neither is healthy.

We must help our children to find a balance between these two extremes, a way to build a self that is both deserving of love and able to offer it selectively to others. But this balance can't be directly taught. The process isn't cognitive or analytical, verbal or intellectual. The process is emotional and experiential.

How do your children see you take care of you?

Do they see you dulling the pain with alcohol or drugs? Mistreating your body or mistreating your mind? Or do they see you getting up and going out to exercise? Saying no at least sometimes to fast food and overeating? Do they see the structures that anchor your life—abiding by the speed limit; attending church; supporting a charity; respecting other people; getting to work on time—as much as they see the structures that you impose on them? Or do they see in you a hypocrite, a person who doesn't practice what she preaches? Will they see this as permission to someday do the same themselves?

Do you let them see that you are finite and flawed and imperfect? That you need other people to refuel you? That you can cry and grieve and then heal? Do you let them see that you trust other people to anchor you? Or do you hide your feelings and failings and humanity behind false pretenses, blame, and rage?

Don't fool yourself: Your kids know the truth. Evolution has programmed them to read your face and your posture, to resonate with your heartbeat and your breathing, to interpret the tension in your muscles, and to respond to the chemical messages in your scent. Even if they can't say it, they know who you are, whether your tank is full, and whether their anchor is secure at a glance.

The Lesson of "No"

Verbs describe actions. Actions must have a start and a stop. Eating and drinking and running. Driving requires pushing on the accelerator at times, and on the brakes at others. Skydiving requires an unwavering certainty when and how to pull the rip cord to stop the fall.

Loving may be an exception, but parenting is not.

Parenting must have its starts and stops or it will break down. Like a firefighter or an emergency room physician, or a 9-1-1 operator, you need to quit when the shift ends, get some sleep and a meal, and take care of yourself, or you will burn out. If you don't go back to your adult anchors to get refueled, you'll have nothing to give later.

This means being able to say "no."

"No, you cannot have another cookie."

"No, you cannot stay out after midnight."

"No" is about limits and boundaries, but it's also about self-care. It tells the child that his need can wait. That it's your turn. That there are limits to what you can and will give, and that you are confident that he'll be fine. That he can wait or that your co-parent can handle it and, in either case, that all is well.

Of course, "no" can provoke rage, particularly when it's unfamiliar. Tantrums and fits and demands may ensue. You may hear screams of "I hate you" (which mean, "I'm really, really mad at you") and guilt trips ("Daddy wouldn't say no!") and threats of blackmail ("If you don't, then I'll run away!"). To give in is to reward these behaviors, and we know that a reward only increases the likelihood that the behavior that earned it will happen again—bigger and badder next time. Why not? It worked.

If the anchor that you provide your children is secure, you'll weather the storm calm and firm and clear. You'll show your child by your example not only that you can manage his feelings, but that you have limits. You know when and how to pull the rip cord and put on the brakes. You can say "no." You are able and invested in taking care of yourself, and someday he will be able to do the same.

COMMUNICATION IMPROVES CONSISTENCY

Parenting is a verb with starts and stops, but it's also a team sport. When you say "no" and step out of the ring, who steps in?

When your husband or wife, intimate partner, next-door neighbor, nanny, babysitter, or your own mom takes over, the transition should be seamless. This means communicating. Agreeing what the rules and rewards are.

When's bedtime?

What chores are expected?

Who's the pediatrician, just in case?

When nurses change shifts in the hospital, they leave one another updated notes on every patient for exactly the same reason. You and your co-parent can do the same. Do your kids go back and forth between two homes? Do they have a regular babysitter or time at Grandma's? Start a communication book now. Before either of you tags out of the ring, update five categories about each child:

1. Eating/sleeping/toileting

2. School/homework

3. Health and medications

4. Friends/social

5. Successes

It's easy to forget that last category, but don't. Taking the time to recognize successes is how we keep the wheel from squeaking.

Practical Pointer:

ALL THINGS IN MODERATION

Taking care of yourself so that you're better able to refuel your kids is a balancing act. At one extreme is the parent who gives endlessly and selflessly to the point of burnout. At the other extreme is the parent who is so over-invested in self-care that his child is neglected. Neither is healthy. No one can tell you how to strike the balance in between. The answer will vary day to day depending on your child's needs, your needs, and the stresses that impact each of you.

One of the additional advantages to making parenting into a team sport is the honest feedback you and your parenting partner can provide one another. The parent who is exhausted but still there on the front line may need to hear, "Take a break. Let me take over for a while." The parent who is consumed with self may need to hear, "Our kids need you. Let's make some changes."

With or without the benefit of this feedback, here are some clues that might help you find your own balance:

1. When was the last time you laughed with your kids? If you can't remember, something's wrong. It's time to change how often you're together or the circumstances when you're together or simply how you're parenting.

2. Can you name your child's teacher(s)? Do you know what he is studying in school? If not, time to check in. Don't intrude, but do wonder aloud. Make an appointment to meet with the teacher. Join the PTA.

3. Can you name your child's best friend? Her favorite band? When was the last time you watched a TV show or movie or YouTube video together? These facts don't require a lot of sleuthing. Even your door-slamming teenager leaves clues everywhere he goes. The page is still up on the computer. The group is featured on his T-shirt.

4. The guys at the gym or the bar or at work (or wherever you go to refuel yourself) don't even know that you have children.

· · · · · · · · · ·

CHAPTER THIRTEEN

IDENTITY DISTORTED

When I look in the mirror,
I try not to see you.

Identity is forged across the span of a lifetime in the crucible of social pressure. This means that you are who you are largely in response to the way that you experience the needs and behavior of the important people in your life. These lessons are seldom communicated directly in words. They're not classroom discussions, pages in a workbook, or the latest app on your phone. They're not even the lectures that parents sometimes give children about "being all that you can be" and how to succeed in life. Rather, these lessons are learned on a physical and emotional level without words and often even without awareness.

You are who you are largely due to your insatiable need to feel held.

There is no greater reward than feeling held tight. Loved. Nurtured. Accepted. Contained. We human beings will choose love rather than food or water and, if a dozen science fiction movies are to be believed, even more than air. The sacrifices we make in order to feel held and to hold those whom we love are the subject of the greatest music and drama known across every medium and every age.

If you've ever taken a psychology course, then you know about

Harry Harlow's experiments with primates.[3] Baby monkeys were given the choice between two wire-frame faux mothers. One provided milk via bottles arranged like breasts. The other was covered in soft cloth but offered no food or drink. The babies could spend as much time with either as they chose. They all chose the textured mother. Food is far less important than feeling held tight.

We are no different. We are intrinsically motivated to be held—to be accepted into the social fabric. We are born with an oceanic sense of self and discover through a million experiments with letting go, how to define self. Where to build the boundaries and how high. We are like stem cells, inherently malleable; shaped by our surroundings to become whatever is needed in order to keep the larger system functioning.

This plan is brilliant and successful if Mom and Dad are healthy, where "healthy" simply means fitting into the larger community. If you fit into family and if family fits into community and if community fits into the world at large, then logic predicts—through the transitive property of social adaptation—that you, too, will fit into the world at large. You'll be deemed "healthy."

And if Mom or Dad is not healthy? If your caregivers' needs and expectations don't align with the needs and expectations of the larger community? If the social pressures that shape your early identity—the ways you learn to get held—are different from those of the larger world? This is one of nature's essential dilemmas and, much more personally, an exquisitely painful problem for many, many people.

The Adultified or Parentified Child

Adults need to be held, even if the need grows less frequent and the fuel goes much farther. But even with bigger gas tanks and better mpg, adults need pit stops just like children—to feel held and reassured. In the best of circumstances, this means turning to an intimate partner, a friend, or a colleague. It might mean a trip home to Mom or a weekend away with the girls or a night out with a brother or

---

3. Curious? See the YouTube video at https://www.youtube.com/watch?v=OrNBEhzjg8I or Google "Harry Harlow monkeys."

sister. Even the familiarity of a fleeting "hello" in passing can feel like an anchor, topping off the tank just enough so that you have more to give to your child.

But some parents make the grave mistake of turning to an immature child for support. Reversing the roles. More or less explicitly asking the child for some of his precious emotional fuel. The parent who prematurely promotes a child into the role of ally or peer, confidant or friend, is "adultifying" the child. The parent who goes even further, making the child into his or her caregiver, is "parentifying" the child.

These are easy mistakes to make. Overwhelmed, exhausted, and bursting at the seams with emotion, Mom comes home and there's Billy, watching TV or playing a video game or doing his homework. He might be five or six, fifteen or sixteen. His age is unimportant. What matters are the roles. Mom is supposed to be the anchor. The gas pump. The thermostat. Her job is to refuel Billy and help him manage his emotions. Her willingness and ability to read and respond to Billy's needs—to hold him tight—is how he feels safe and secure.

There is absolutely nothing wrong with Mom feeling overwhelmed or even letting Billy know this in moderation. He needs to see that she's human in order to allow himself to be human as well. To know that she can cry or rage or worry and that he's safe all the while. To learn that strong emotion can be managed. The problem occurs when Mom asks Billy to manage her emotions.

Remember that Billy, like all of us, is eager to win love and approval; in this case, from his mom. He wants to feel held tight. If listening to Mom rant about the boss or cry about the bills or complain about how the guy she went out with last night tried to grope her gets him held, then that's what he'll do. And he'll do it with equal parts pride and confusion. He'll nod his head and pat her back and hug her while she sobs, even though he knows nothing about bosses or bills or groping. If getting her medicine or pouring her another beer or cleaning up her vomit or tucking her into bed gets him held, then he'll gladly become her best friend or caregiver.

Later, his experience as Mom's helper and best friend will shape his personality. His expectations for other relationships will shift. He'll become a caregiver to others and an enabler. He'll compromise his own needs in order to care for others. He'll often feel used and discarded. He may see himself as disposable, as unimportant, and he won't know why. If he succeeds in school, he might become a nurse or a therapist, and he might even be good at what he does, but he'll do it for the wrong reasons and then he'll burn out.

Adultification and parentification can cost a child the opportunity to learn how to value and care for himself. These experiences can leave the boundaries of identity fragile. The lesson is that you can only be loved for what you give, and you can never give enough. Looking back, years later, empty and sad, Billy may discover that he is angry at Mom for having relied on him—he was just a little boy!—and for cheating him out of his childhood.

The problem is that children generally enjoy being adultified and parentified. The role makes them feel needed and valuable, valued and held. They feel special, sometimes because a selfish and needy parent has told them exactly that. But they win these misplaced kudos by surrendering their anchor in order to become one.

Parents rationalize these role reversals as if there could ever be a good reason to treat a child like a peer or a parent. "He's an old soul," they say, or, "He deserves to know." Mistaking a child's verbal strengths or social skills for maturity, they explain, "He can deal with it."

And then there are those who mistake a child's physical development for genuine maturity, opening the door not only to adultification and parentification but to sexual contact as well. In these few, extreme instances, a child endures horrific, identity-altering abuse at the hands of an isolated and needy and disturbed parent who teaches him that this is how to feel held.

Many Maturities

Maturity is not a single measure like height or weight. We each mature in different areas of functioning at different rates. Physical, cognitive, emotional, and social maturities, for example, can all be quite distinct.

But beware: Physically and socially mature children look and sound impressive, but their size and expressive skills can sometimes cover up lags in emotional maturity. The adultified or parentified child, for example, knows how to fit in among adults and may even crave the opportunity, but she can't sleep at night because the information she gets from her mom is more than she can manage.

The Infantilized Child

For some parents, the need to feel needed is never more completely satisfied than it is while caring for a baby. These parents—often very young mothers who feel that they, themselves, were never mothered—mistake the baby's clingy, crying, sucking, wide-eyed wonder as emotional fuel. This parent feels loved and lovable, valued and competent and fulfilled, so long as the baby needs her.

The "infantilized" child is taught to never let go. His neediness and dependence are rewarded by a disturbed parent's distorted needs. Like adultified and parentified children, the infantilized child relishes his role in his mother's life, no matter that his development quickly falls behind that of his peers, and no matter that he fits less well into the larger world with each passing year.

The infantilized child is sometimes mistaken as socially or emotionally or cognitively delayed, as autistic or overwhelmingly anxious or otherwise in need of intense supports. As long as he remains in the infantilizing environment, these observations may be correct, but they are effects, not causes. They are the way that a disturbed parent gets her selfish needs fulfilled.

In one bizarre and uncommon twist on this theme, a needy parent finds fulfillment when her child is ill, even to the extent of intentionally making him sick. Doctors are consulted, tests are performed, emergency rooms and hospitals are involved, all to solve the mystery and support the helpless parent's desperate pleas. For this parent, the professionals' interest and attention are mistaken for feeling held, refueling her need to keep the child ill. This is called factitious disorder or Munchausen syndrome by proxy.

PUSH ME, PULL YOU

The child who fails to launch likely needs both a push and a pull. In many cases, one won't work without the other.

The push comes from behind in the form of the parent's reassurance that it's okay to be apart and, in particularly that she—the parent—will be fine. Offering these words insincerely will only exacerbate the problem. This child reads his parent's emotions like Braille.

The pull must come from his next anchor. Someone or someplace safe and familiar and welcoming. The more safe and familiar—structured—the more effective the pull.

And transitional objects will help along the way. These are things that make the absent parent's security portable and present for the child as well as things that make the absent child's security immediate for the parent.

Failure to Launch

We let go of our emotional anchors a million times between birth and death. Each instance brings with it the same seesaw mix of anxiety and opportunity. Anytime that the terror outweighs the adventure, we cling tight to that which is secure and familiar.

The healthy child toddles forth in greater and greater arcs of exploration, confident that his anxiety can be managed, that the anchor rope is secure. He carries in his arms or his wallet or his mind bits and pieces of the security that he associates with Mom or Dad, his emotional anchors, and these refuel him. They give him confidence to keep exploring until he can find a group or club or gang and then an intimate partner to hold him tight. To anchor him.

Adultified, parentified and infantilized children, however, are the anchors. A parent's selfish and misplaced needs keep the anchor rope short; it makes growing up and growing apart too scary, not because the world is threatening, but because autonomy means loss. These children's identities are so enmeshed with their parents' well-being that they might never truly separate. In the words of a popular contemporary movie, this is failure to launch.

This failure is not about the child's ability—at least, not at first. When cognitive or medical differences restrict a child's capacity to separate, we do everything we can to give them as much autonomy as possible. The privacy and freedoms that they are able to safely manage. To let them go in every way that they are able.

And this is not about money. College loans and the vagaries of the job market, fixed incomes, medical expenses, and the economy in general force lots of kids to live at home and lots of parents to move in with their adult children. Parents and children can share a space and a budget and can even become co-parents to a child's child while remaining mature and separate people, each with their own lives. Each with their own anchors apart from or in addition to the other.

The child who fails to launch may not have the confidence and security to leave home, to move away from the anchor that Mom and Dad provide, and to affiliate with groups or clubs or cliques like way stations on the way out of his parents' orbit. Instead, the gravity of his parents' needs and his anxiety keep him home, functional and perhaps even happy within a very small container, but lacking the skills to manage in almost any other environment.

Practical Pointer:

CUTTING THE ANCHOR LINE?

When a parent gets her needs met through her child, the child carries the burden of knowing that letting go means harming Mom. He may not be able to put it in words, but the implicit emotional message is "Mom depends on me. I can't leave her." This is an impossible and destructive bind for any child at any age. It either means becoming consumed by the parent's pathological need or finding the emotional strength to break free and to tolerate the rage and despair that will likely follow.

When specialized therapies and carefully crafted court orders and well-intended social services fail to rescue the infantilized, adulti-fied, or parentified child, sometimes the anchor rope needs to be cut. The child needs simply to be removed from the dependent parent's care at least temporarily while multiple convergent therapies try to help all involved. In extreme cases documented in U.S. and Canadian courts, abrupt removal into the care of a healthy parent sometimes proves to be exactly the right remedy, but other times is associated with tragic outcomes.

Unfortunately, we don't yet know which remedies are right for which children. We do know, however, that it's better to respond sooner rather than later and that the response will require the concerted and collaborative effort of numerous health care professionals.

. . . .

CHAPTER FOURTEEN

PERSONALITY ORDERED AND DISORDERED

If beauty is in the eye of the beholder,
then so too are kindness and evil,
generosity and selfishness,
virtue and vice.

If identity is how you see yourself in the mirror, personality is how you see others. It is the constellation of fears and hopes, wishes and needs, borne of nurture and seasoned by nature, that you cast upon the people in your world.

Our lifelong experiences of holding tight and letting go lay the foundation for self in the context of others' caring. We discover who we are in large part by discovering how other people respond to us. What emerges over a lifetime is a more or less coherent identity defined in large part by expectations about relationships.

Am I deserving of love?

Can I rely on others?

Can other people tolerate my anger? My anxiety? My neediness?

How much do I have to give, in order to get?

Personality is the lens through which we perceive the social and emotional environment. It is shaded and colored and scarred by experience, focused and then refocused by here-and-now influences like medication and hormones, diet and nutrition, exercise and stress, and the media we consume. It is the eye through which the beholder interprets not only beauty, but acceptance and rejection, self-esteem, love and loss as well.

Like any lens, personality can become very distorted.

Experience affects development. The effect is usually gradual, the way that a river slowly erodes its banks. Prenatal alcohol exposure, for example, can induce a permanent disruption of social, emotional, physical, and cognitive functioning over time known as fetal alcohol syndrome. Preschool lead poisoning can cause learning and sensory problems and even death.

On the other hand, some experiences can produce an abrupt and dramatic effect on identity and personality: Surviving a school shooting. Living through a terrorist attack or a natural disaster. Neglect or abuse. A devastating car accident, a dog bite, or a profound emotional loss.

Of course, in the best of circumstances, positive experiences build a robust and adaptive personality the same way that snowflakes can be packed together to become a smiling snowman. Healthy nutrition, exercise, proper medical care, good sleep, and rewarding relationships combine to become something sturdy and coherent, but still flexible and adaptive.

This is personality well ordered. The sum total of experiences from conception through the present is what yields a self able and willing to get needs met and to recognize and meet the needs of others. Of course, this looks very different at age three versus thirteen versus thirty, but the goal is the same no matter the age. Healthy personality is the ability to fit into the social environment. It is the willingness and ability to balance giving and getting, holding tight and letting go.

And personality disorder? In one view, the term is an oxymoron. A contradiction within itself. Personality cannot be *disordered* if it emerges as an adaptation to its environment. If our social and emotional expectations evolve in response to real and ongoing social pressures, then even the most rigid and aggressive, wishy-washy passive, or needy and demanding personality must be okay because it works.

Or worked. Once upon a time every personality worked in the sense of fitting in to a particular environment. But if that person leaves that environment or if the environment changes, what once fit becomes a misfit.

Get out your rolling pin and flatten a ball of dough. Grab any cookie cutter and impress its shape in the middle of the powdery, pale mass. The result may be misshapen and asymmetrical and just plain bizarre, but I guarantee you that it fits right back into the hole from which it came.

Now step back from the flour-strewn countertop and take a longer view. From this distance, it's possible to see that personality can be disordered to the extent that an adaptation to one environment may be ill-suited to another. Your odd-shaped cookie worked in the context of the dough from which it was cut, but will be discarded by the baker or overlooked by his customers. What worked in one context, failed in another and, in this instance, there's no room for growth. The cookie can't change. It's inanimate. It can't adjust its limbs or learn to say "please" or wait its turn; it can't cooperate with a co-cookie or learn how to nurture a crumb.

The media have given us scores of dramatic (and usually fictitious) examples of personality ordered and disordered. "Tarzan" has become a cultural archetype, the story of a man well adapted to one environment but adrift in the larger society. A similar story is retold today in a beautiful children's book called *Stellaluna*, the tale of a bat raised among birds and then returned to her own species.

The Munsters was a 1960s comedy about a family of monster-like people who barely tolerated their misfit niece, Marilyn, a stunning and intelligent teenager who thought herself hideous and bizarre; a freak. When the family ventured into the larger world, however, it was always the Frankenstein-like father, Herman Munster, who scared the neighbors away.

The tragedy of misfit personality—personality disordered—is played out in real life all around us every day. Seeing people with personality disorders for who they are rather than just reacting to them takes a lot of patience and maturity. The self-centered man at the office, the angry and super-critical neighbor, the sad and self-effacing woman at the library—these people trigger strong emotional reactions, but they're just trying to fit in.

CHANGING SOCIAL CONTEXT

Because we know that identity and personality are cut from the fabric of relationships, changing personality often requires a change of relationships. Very practical steps to relocate, to enroll a child in a boarding school or asleep-away camp, can be helpful and sometimes necessary.

This is nowhere more obvious than among alcoholics and addicts. When a community supports and encourages addictive behaviors as the way to fit in, be accepted, and feel held, quitting is near impossible. Making the giant leap into a non-using community that values and rewards sobriety is often a necessary and critical step toward achieving and sustaining abstinence.

This is true not only for addictions to alcohol, cocaine, and meth but also with addictions to video gaming, pornography, shopping, and gambling. Parents who want to minimize their child's screen time, for example, may need to work with others in the community (the school's PTA or the local scouting troop, for example) to achieve real and lasting change.

Reactive Attachment Disorder (RAD)

Children abandoned at birth to spend their earliest years in impersonal, institutional settings may get their physical needs met, but their experience of feeling held tight and let go can become profoundly distorted. When care is impersonal and inconstant—when you're fed and bathed and dressed by another random face in an assembly line; when you are emotionally unanchored—you're at grave risk of becoming socially indiscriminant. Everyone seems the same. Children with RAD either fail to become drips, undifferentiated from those around them, their boundaries sieve-like; or they construct identities within boundaries that are vault-like, rejecting care from everyone, all the time. Either of these two outcomes may be adaptive and necessary to survival in an Eastern European orphanage, but both are terribly maladaptive in the world at large.

RAD is both a tragic diagnosis and an excellent illustration of how early experience can shape how we perceive and engage the social world. Although RAD itself is not considered a personality disorder *per se*, the flaws in these children's essential identity and, therefore, in their personality resonate through their entire lives. They are left vulnerable to innumerable social and emotional (as well as legal, educational, and physical health) dangers, relatively incapable of ever holding others or feeling held. Having never known an emotional anchor, they might never be able to become one.

Personality Disordered

The best formula we have for raising psychologically healthy children is prescribed in hundreds of places, including here in this book. The details may vary, but the essential message is the same: Hold tight and let go. Ensure that the child has an anchor, that he feels bounded, that his anxiety can be controlled and his rage contained. These and similar ideas are insurance, but by no means a guarantee. Genetics and experience can throw even the healthiest individual off one developmental path and onto another.

Corrective emotional experiences can help most who are lost find their way back. This may take many different forms: Psychotherapy. The constancy of a loving and responsive teacher, coach, or mentor. Establishing a relationship with a grandparent, uncle, neighbor, or friend who becomes an emotional anchor. Even a pet can become part of the solution.

There are, however, variables of both nature and nurture that over and over again prove to be critical risk factors for developing personality disorders. RAD represents one extreme. Others may be more subtle but ultimately no less damaging. When these factors are mixed, singly or in combination with genetic vulnerabilities, physical illness, and the stresses associated with poverty or natural disaster, the lens through which a child views self and others can become profoundly distorted.

We know that children who have *at least one* healthy anchor among two or more caregivers can be okay even in the midst of horrific trauma. It also stands to reason that children who have *only one* anchor are at greater risk than those who have two or more. Like the skydiver who has no backup chute or the proverbial farmer who keeps all of his eggs in one basket, this child has only one chance to get it right.

We know, too, that experiencing emotional, physical, and sexual abuse can induce guilt and shame and rage and sadness, which themselves can complicate identity and confound relatedness. When the perpetrators of these heinous acts are also the people who are supposed to keep you safe, the trauma of assault can be lost in the shadow of the trauma of betrayal. Insults can be forgiven. Bruises and broken bones can heal. But learning to trust others when the person you're supposed to be able to trust the most has harmed you can be exponentially harder.

What happens to identity and personality when holding tight means getting hurt?

What happens when the boundaries you're building while you're apart are breached upon your return?

What happens if you're praised for letting go today but chastised for doing the same tomorrow?

What happens when the person responsible for helping you manage your anxiety causes it?

As parents, we are supposed to be our children's anchors. Their port in the storm and secure base. The thermostat that regulates arousal, and the model to be internalized and emulated. If you recognize and respect this precious and profound responsibility, you have a good chance to set your son or daughter on a path toward health; to lay a psychological foundation for the later development of an identity and a personality that are robust and balanced. Flexible and adaptive. Sensitive and responsive. Able to hold tight and let go.

But if you selfishly fail to anchor your child—if you fail to protect him from the storm, if you teach him that holding hurts or that letting go means loss, if you blindly cast your own smoldering and septic childhood needs where they don't belong—you risk corrupting your child's opportunity to ever know himself and relate to others. You risk scarring, perhaps permanently, the lens through which he will view all relationships to come.

Worse still, the neglectful parent—consumed by addiction or selfishness; depression or anxiety; ignorance, immaturity, or the voices in her head—is simply missing in action. Absent. Certainly you know the panic that blossoms in your chest when you return to a crowded parking lot and can't find your car. What if you turned onto your street and couldn't find your home? What if you woke up every morning uncertain whether there would be food or clothing or a roof over your head? This is perhaps a kernel of the neglected child's constant and intense anxiety. She has been cast adrift without anchor. Abuse is never good, but it may be less destructive of identity and personality than neglect. At least the abusive parent is acknowledging the child's existence.

Personality (Dis)ordered by Degree

Psychiatry has many times attempted to catalog the differences among adult personality constellations the way that Audubon cataloged birds or Dewey cataloged books. These attempts have been complicated by our very limited and subjective understanding, by prejudice, politics, and passions. Despite a recent move toward more scientific and empirically determined categories, we still don't know what combination of risk factors are most likely to create any particular distortion of personality or, far more critically, how to correct them. We are nevertheless left with a collection of labels—borderline personality disorder, narcissistic personality disorder, obsessive-compulsive personality disorder, or schizotypal personality disorder, to name just a few—that get thrown around like stones by people who don't seem to realize that they, too, live in glass houses.

Broken bones are painful and often inconvenient, but they are diagnostically simple. There is a yes-or-know, literally black-and-white

X-ray distinction to be made. Either the bone is broken or it's not. Appendicitis is a little less clear. Pneumonia and multiple sclerosis and Lyme disease and syphilis each have their own telltale markers.

As the stepchild of medicine, psychiatry has tried and failed to approach matters of personality and relatedness in the same way. Thus, we refer to "mental illness" as if it were as discrete and diagnosable as a fractured limb, as quantifiable as a blood count, or as objective as a CAT scan. I suppose there are a few, very extreme psychological conditions that can be diagnosed in this way, but more generally, it's all a matter of perception and degree.

My experience as a clinician has led me to think of personality in terms of two specific variables: distress and dysfunction. The former is a subjective measure—the view from the inside looking out. It asks what hurts and how much and when. The latter is the objective measure—the view from the outside looking in. Dysfunction asks which among the many common components of adult relatedness you are able to manage. Communication? Frustration tolerance? Delay of gratification? Ability to compromise? Provide support? Assert strong feelings? Care for your children?

I find that tracking these two variables over time—as a matter of history in response to significant past events, and through the future in response to specific interventions—is a commonsense and practical way to communicate with and about a person without labeling and without stigma.

In fact, psychiatry's most recent catalog of personal disorder diagnoses includes both the conventional diagnostic definitions and a new, alternative model.[4] In this model, personality functioning is described along four continuous variables offered here and defined in the terms of this book:

- **Identity:** The subjective experience that one is bounded; a drip fully emerged from the ocean in which it was once con-

---

4. American Psychiatric Association, *The Diagnostic and Statistical Manual of Mental Disorders,* fifth edition (Arlington, VA: American Psychiatric Publishing, 2013). See page 761 for an introduction to the "alternative model."

tained. A person who is willing and able to accept pride of success and responsibility for failure, to offer others praise and criticism, and to accept the same, in return, all without compromising identity.

- **Self-direction:** The ability and willingness to move away from the familiar toward a desired goal, to internalize the security that makes the effort manageable, to tolerate frustration along the way, and to ask for support when necessary.

- **Empathy:** The capacity to see others and their needs untainted by one's own. To understand how one's behavior is likely to affect others and how others' behavior affects oneself.

- **Intimacy:** The capacity for reciprocal emotional exchange. The ability to express a need to be held, to accept another person's holding, and to offer the same in return.

Thinking in terms of these four continuous dimensions, the conventional categories of personality disorder can begin to be cast as reasonable adaptations to unreasonable caregiving environments— disfigured cookies with the will and the opportunity to make changes in order to better fit on the baker's shelf. Borderline personality disorder, for example, can now be described as a developmental outcome characterized by impoverished self-image, an inability to work toward goals, a very limited ability to recognize others' needs as distinct from one's own, unstable and extreme moods that impact others, and intense, unstable relationships. As a child, this person might never have had even one stable emotional anchor, might never have had the security of knowing that separation is followed by reunion, and therefore might never have built the boundaries that define a healthy self and personality.

Recognizing these specific deficits and their origins both diminishes stigma and helps to prescribe remedies. Disordered or maladaptive personalities might be bandaged by learning and practicing new skills: How to greet someone in the workplace. How to recognize and redirect frustration. How to read and respond to nonverbal social cues. But the real remedy for the ill underneath the gauze and tape requires that the individual establish new and healthier anchors. The person needs better fitting structures that can be internalized so he can construct more appropriate boundaries, a healthier identity and personality.

Practical Pointer:

ONE KIND OF HELP—DIALECTICAL BEHAVIOR THERAPY

Dialectical behavior therapy (DBT) is one of the more popular contemporary treatments for some personality and substance abuse disorders. DBT is a type of cognitive behavioral therapy.

DBT emphasizes mindfulness and cultivating a non-judgmental worldview. It helps participants to identify the thoughts, feelings, and events that trigger "emotional dysregulation"—the flaws in the lens of personality that distort an ambiguous or even a benign event into something feared or threatening. DBT helps reset the emotional thermostat and provides a very specific and reassuring experience of being held tight.

· · · · · · · · · ·

CHAPTER FIFTEEN

BROKEN TRIANGLES

Love divided by two
is simple math.
Love divided by three
is a high wire balancing act.
Don't try it without a net.

Bouncing Baby Bobby arrived healthy and fit, with the lungs of a yodeler and the grip of a sumo wrestler. He was round and bald and watchful. Billy thought of him as a little Buddha. Honey thought of him as her life.

She'd left her job when she was too round to fit behind her desk. That cost the couple half their income. So Billy got a part-time job three evenings a week in addition to his full-time day job. It didn't close the budget gap, which was actually looking more and more like a black hole—sucking money in as the endless avalanche of baby needs grew—but shower gifts helped; their parents helped. Nonetheless, the stress was building.

Honey was exhausted and irritable before Bobby was born. Thirty-six hours of labor didn't help. Billy didn't help, either. The unspoken seesaw balance of give and take that had once worked so well between them was shifting dramatically. They were both running on fumes as beautiful Baby Bobby entered the drama, screaming, stage right. Blissfully ignorant of everything except breast and bottom. Awash in his ocean of me-here-now self.

Many—perhaps even most—adult relationships manage the change from two to three adequately, but none do so without scars. For everything gained, there is at least one loss, and often more. The success of the transition relies on the new parents' health and maturity: The primitive foundation each laid in infancy. The emotional thermostat's ability to manage extreme stress. The boundaries defining identity. The perceptions and expectations built into personality. The number and nature of secondary emotional supports. But for all of these vague and complex considerations, Baby Bobby's arrival really is just another instance of letting go.

Once upon a time, a hundred years before and a dozen chapters ago, Billy had been the baby. He sat on his mother's lap in the middle of an unfamiliar room, holding her tight. Refueled, calmed by her steady heartbeat and respirations, confident in her casual grasp, he could feel his anxiety settle. He scanned and then fussed and then was let go. Off he toddled, discovering self, confident that Mom would airlift him to safety at the first sign of distress.

Now adult Billy's been let go again. The physical distance between him and his anchor—his wife—may be tiny, but the emotional distance seems huge. Honey's there, just on the other side of the bed, but there's a chasm between them, and its name is Bobby. He turns to make eye contact, to hold her hand, to be reassured and to reassure her, but she's not there. She's absorbed in their beautiful little boy, as she must be.

Honey's experience is different. She, too, has been let go. Her emotional anchor is grouchy and tired and drinking too much. He's always at one job or another, and she's grateful but lonely too. She's had her own mom and her girlfriends around to refuel her, but she's also had the bizarre and wonderful and totally incomparable experience of growing a new human being inside of her.

Over the months that her shadow became wider than it was high, she had a growing sense of synchrony or symmetry or synergy. Two-ness. She'd tried and failed to share it with Billy. His hand on the spot where the baby kicked and his ear to her distended tummy didn't even come close. It was inevitably outside of him. Foreign. An idea rather than an emotion. More than the medical facts of what was happening inside of her, her selfness was somehow shifting. Slipping. There was an echo of her, inside of her.

She'd feared *Alien* ripping its way out of her chest. She'd gotten Mini-Me.

Her love for Billy was no less, but her love for Baby Bobby was profound. His happiness was her happiness. His cries were hers. Nursing him was the utter bliss of coming home. Reconnecting. Floating. The feeling was . . . oceanic. The act refilled her far more than it drained her.

Here the story diverges like the fate of Schrödinger's cat. In one reality, the family of three finds balance. A triangle of complementary if unequal roles, needs, and resources. Billy and Honey discover new ways to be refueled by one another and, in the process, become better able to manage their stress. Their intimate adult relationship takes on the additional dimension of co-parenting. They become an efficient tag team, refueling one another even as each refuels their baby. They discover how to communicate and cooperate, and gradually they refine the consistency of their parenting practices.

In this reality, mother and father together weave a safety net that catches and holds their son. They establish limits and follow through with consequences, finding ways to reward Bobby's successes rather than wait to oil the wheel when it squeaks. They establish both boundaries that define space and routines that define time. During the years ahead, these are the structures that Bobby—no longer a bouncing baby—will internalize and fall back on as he defines his own identity and personality; as he ventures off clutching a transitional object; as he establishes transitional affiliations; and as he finds new anchors in his adult world.

But you know that story. Billy lived it. Perhaps you're fortunate enough to have lived it, too. It's the other story that demands our attention:

Sex can make one out of two, and then three out of one. But not always. Sometimes the triangle breaks, creating unbalanced and unhealthy alliances. In this all-too-common reality, Honey's pregnancy and Bobby's birth have pushed Billy away. He's not only physically separated by working two jobs; he's emotionally left out. Like the skinny kid with acne who is never picked for the team, Billy sees his wife and his son laughing and playing and sleeping together. He sees the baby clinging to what he once thought of as his, and he gets it, but he resents it.

It might take days or months or years, but Billy and Honey eventually stop turning to each other for emotional fuel. They find new anchors. Honey has her mom and her friends. Billy has the guys at work and his friends at the bar.

There's no room for Billy in the big bed anymore, so he sleeps on the couch.

Honey's too tired to go out at night, so Billy calls a friend.

Meals at home are mushy green, orange, or yellow and come in four-ounce jars, so he eats out. Emotion and misunderstanding accumulate like debris washed up on the shore between Honey and Billy, becoming a speed bump and then a hill and then a mountain that cannot be climbed, even with the help of the professionals they hire to show them the way.

Sometimes there's a last straw: an argument, a secret, a lover, a suspicion, a shove. Sometimes not. But there always is letting go: a divestment, a withdrawal of dependence and trust. The anchor line, frayed and unraveled, breaks. Falling too fast, the primary parachute is jettisoned because it opened tattered and torn.

The end of an intimate relationship can feel like being cast adrift. It's the intellectualized, lawyer-laden, public and profound panic that Bouncing Baby Billy felt when he looked back to discover that Mom was gone. It's a grieving process like any other, complete with its own stages of denial, anger, bargaining, depression, and—hopefully, eventually—acceptance. It's a test of emotional resilience and resourcefulness.

The Complications of Divorce

Back in the bad old days, fathers literally owned their wives and children, no different from owning their cows and bales of hay. Sons were valued for their work. Daughters were bargaining chips to be sold off to an adjoining farm or an adjoining kingdom to cement alliances and to create more sons, all in a process called marriage. Fathers still "give away" their daughters, but the union has ceased to be a matter of mergers and has become, instead, a means of ensuring monogamy and a public declaration of unquenchable and undying and mutual love. Marriage is the formal, public, and government-sanctioned act that ties you to a new emotional anchor.

Untying this knot has never been easy. For centuries (and still today in some cultures and religions) it was nearly impossible. But in the last fifty years the pendulum has swung in the other direction. Some would say that we marry and divorce today almost as easily as we buy and sell cars. Tired of one? Discovered that you got a lemon? Totaled it in a wreck? Trade it in for another, newer model.

Unless there's children. That same pendulum has swung back and forth through the history of post-divorce custody practices. In the bad old days, the wife who dared take her children from her husband was committing theft. She was stealing his property. Years later the tables turned. Mom was the only and best parent able to care for children still in their "tender years." The politically motivated, gender-blind movement for equality pushed forward, ignoring biology, suggesting at one time that the post-divorce ratio of parenting should be no different from the pre-separation division of care and, more recently, that a fifty-fifty split would settle the parents' differences, and perhaps even serve the best interests of the children.

To argue about the virtues of these various solutions misses the point. Divorce doesn't harm children. Parents do.

Practical Pointer:

IT'S NOT YOUR TIME; IT'S THE CHILD'S TIME IN YOUR CARE

Many jurisdictions assume that an equal split of the child's time between the parents' care serves the best interests of the children. Although some form of a fifty-fifty split may make sense, this assumption generally suits the needs of the contentious parents first and foremost.

If and how a child's care should be split between his parents' homes can be an explosive subject. Family law attorneys and judges, guardians ad litem, and specially trained custody evaluators can usually be helpful. At issue is not the parents' wishes or even the child's wishes, but the child's needs and how each parent's social, emotional, intellectual, and material resources can meet those needs.

Perhaps most critical when discussing the future allocation of parenting rights and responsibilities, however, are the structures established to keep the kids out of the middle of the adult conflict. For example:

1. Never make the child into a messenger, courier, or spy between homes.

2. Don't ask the child to keep secrets with one parent from the other.

3. Don't ask the child to choose between parents.

4. Find a balance between the number of transitions between homes the child must endure each week on one hand versus how long she has to be away from each parent on the other.

Read more in my book *Keeping Kids Out of the Middle.*

· · · · · · · · · ·

CHAPTER SIXTEEN

CAUGHT IN THE MIDDLE

*There can be no choice between
inhaling and exhaling.
I can hold my breath only so long,
and then I must do both.*

Some children live in what feels like a war zone. They are forced to choose between parents who are too immature, too selfish, too needy, too angry, and too disturbed to understand that although adult love can end, parent-child love must not. Conscripted, this child learns that if he wants to feel held by Mom, he must reject Dad. That if he wants to feel held by Dad, he must reject Mom. He must pick sides, declare his allegiance, and join in a battle in which there can be no victor, only victims.

Secured by two anchors close at hand, he might feel more confident. Secured by two anchors miles apart, he is torn in two.

The child who is triangulated into his parents' conflict has a very different experience of holding tight and letting go. He migrates between disparate worlds on a schedule that might suit his parents or comply with the ruling of a judge he will never know and who knows him not at all. His life is divided into days colored blue and days colored red on the calendar hanging on mom's freezer, and then there's the tense exchanges where the two colors meet.

Blue days are okay. Bobby knows his bedtime and where to find the breakfast cereal in the morning, which dog growls and which one likes to play. He knows if he gets stuck on a math problem or scared at night that he can call out to Dad and Dad will come running. His stepmom is mean, but that's okay, 'cuz they have a pool in the summer, Xbox in the winter, and a game room in the basement.

Red days are okay too. Mom's house is smaller, just an apartment really. But Bobby's got all of his stuffies in bed with him 'cuz sometimes Mom can't hear his bad dreams. He can go to sleep whenever he wants as long as he's quiet and doesn't bother Mom and her boyfriend in their room. She's got an iPad he can use sometimes, his best friend lives down the hall, and it's a lot closer to school so he can sleep in, even though sometimes she makes him walk to school.

Wednesdays are change days, and Bobby hates change. He wakes up in the red house and tries to hide under the stuffed animals, but Mom yanks him out anyway. She tells him to pack up to go to "the other house." Not "Dad's house" or even "your father's house" or the "blue house." She's always sad on Wednesdays and wants lots of extra cuddles, even though he just wants to go to school.

Bobby picks one stuffy to go with him, shoves it in his back-and-forth bag, and kisses Mom good-bye in the car pool line. She puts her heart bracelet on his ankle under his sock like she does every Wednesday and reminds him that she wants it back soon.

Dad's there after school, or sometimes his stepmom when Dad's busy. They stop for ice cream on the way back to the blue house and talk, but never about Mom. Every time Daddy calls her "Honey," he says it like it's a swear word, and Bobby feels the chain around his ankle itch and burn. He can call Mom from the blue house, but only when Dad's listening, and when Dad's listening his face gets all twisty tight, so Bobby doesn't call. He doesn't really eat, either. He's never really hungry on Wednesdays but he's always sleepy. Dad says this is because "*Honey*" doesn't give him a bedtime. Bobby thinks it's really because Wednesdays are so hard.

Caught in a war zone between parents, letting go means loss, not discovery. Building the boundaries of self is a luxury this child cannot afford. He doesn't have the security even of knowing who will be there to hold him tight when he returns.

For you and me, this is the difference between leaving for a day at work, confident that you'll return home to a warm meal, a soft bed, and welcoming arms, versus leaving to travel to a distant country. You might know all the customs and languages and dress, the rules and roles and geography. You might remember to change your watch to the correct time zone, but the change is exhausting. Even that would be okay if you had a chance to settle in—unpack, get over the jet lag, get used to the new routine—but, to live in Bobby's world, you have make the return trip just a day or two later.

New York to Shanghai and back, twice every week for the rest of your childhood.

Desperate to feel held tight, anchored, and contained, Bobby has very few options. He can blame himself for the adult conflict and, in so doing, preserve his idealized image of his very flawed parents. He can maintain irrational fantasies of reunion long after both parents remarry, even long after both have died. He can compromise his identity and become a chameleon. Or he can compromise his security by becoming a polarized or an alienated child.

The Chameleon Child

The chameleon child resolves the pressure of being forced to take sides by taking both. In the red home, Bobby becomes red. In the blue home, he becomes blue. He says and does in each home whatever it is that gets him held and reassured there. It doesn't matter that what he says to Mom on Tuesday could be the opposite of what he says to Dad on Thursday. By becoming a chameleon, he clings to both anchor ropes, always hiding one from the other.

The chameleon child is always looking outside of himself, never in. He is exquisitely well attuned to his environment and painfully ignorant of his self. By devoting his energy to fitting in, he neglects the opportunity to build boundaries defining an identity. But that's okay, because he lives in a world in which having an opinion—a coherent and bounded self—would cost him love. After all, he's seen firsthand how anger ends love.

Chameleon children are socially facile and fun. By definition, they fit in. These children tend to be the class clown, the life of the party, the entertainer or the politician. Often, they grow up to become narcissists—glad-handing, self-aggrandizing people who constantly demand affirmation, attention, affection, admiration, and love. They can never get enough emotional fuel because there is a hole in the bottom of their tank. Ironically, psychotherapy may seem to cause a chameleon child to have more problems, not fewer. Growing a self causes friction.

Unfortunately, Bobby's chameleon-like behavior will only exacerbate the conflict that he is trying to manage. Because his parents don't communicate and each makes the mistake of taking his every word at face value, his desperate attempt to be loved will drive his parents further apart.

The Polarized Child

This child resolves the pressures of his parents' war by picking sides. Aligning with one and rejecting the other. Clinging to one anchor and cutting the rope on the other. This outcome would seem to make tremendous sense—it relieves the pressure that might otherwise corrupt his identity—except there is no good reason he can't have the benefit of both.

Children become aligned with one parent and reject the other for many reasons. Some are as trivial as who offers the larger allowance, the greater freedoms, and the fewest rules. Others are developmentally expectable, even if they're not always acceptable: A school-aged boy's need for a male role model. An embarrassed and self-conscious girl who needs her mother's special help during puberty.

Some reasons are as powerful as they are invisible. A child's fears of Dad's neighbor's new dog, a teenager's crush on the girl next door, a little boy's parentified worry that his mom won't take her medicine while he's away, or a little girl's worry that she has to protect a half-sister from their abusive father.

And some of the pressures that polarize a child are just plain selfish: The mom who turns her son's room into a den because the child

144

is so rarely there and now he has no place to come home to. The dad who treats his daughter like a Cinderella slave, a second-class citizen who must serve his new wife and stepchildren.

Or the parent who alienates.

Billy alienates Baby Bobby from his mom, Honey, in various ways: When he says her name with an angry emphasis. When he isn't careful that Bobby is really asleep and not listening to his drunken expletives about the woman who abandoned him. And when he simply tells Bobby that his mother is a wench.

The concept of alienation has had a tortured history. Back in the days of chattel, when the father owned his wife and children, a husband could sue a third party for undermining his relationship with his woman. In the late 1990s, the term was reinvigorated by a psychiatrist who diagnosed children with a self-proclaimed syndrome that occurred when a mother undermined a child's relationship with his father. Today we use the term more narrowly and more cautiously to describe one of the many dynamics that can occur within a conflicted family system.

The alienated child has chosen sides in his parents' war. In his view, one parent is all good and the other is all bad. It doesn't matter that his black-and-white, all-or-nothing perspective is impossible, that his reasoning is hollow, that his angry words are an obvious echo of the aligned parent's words, or that there is no objective evidence to support his claims. True, Dad yelled at him, but he was trying to be heard in a rock concert. True, Mom didn't pick him up after school, but she was in the emergency room at the time.

Solutions

It is always better to repair the cause than simply to bandage the effect. If your house is flooding, you can bail, or you can turn off the water supply leading to the broken pipe. If you're shivering with cold, you can put on a sweater, or you can go indoors. And if your child is suffering, you can medicate him or enroll him in psychotherapy or hire lawyers, or you can address the problem that is causing him pain so that he can heal.

If your answer is to point your finger at your co-parent, that's the problem. Not a solution. It may be true that you can't fix this problem alone, but you must fix your part of it. Take the high road. No matter what you believe your co-parent might be doing, do what you know is best for your child. Protect his need to be safe—to feel anchored and secure and contained—long before you protect your dignity. You're the adult. Go get refueled elsewhere. That's what friends and therapists and church and lovers are for.

Practical Pointer:
TAKE THE HIGH ROAD

Many parents who see their children suffer as a result of adult conflict feel helpless in the belief that the other parent's behavior can't be changed. While it's certainly true that no one can change another person's behavior, there's no reason for helplessness. Every parent can and must take the high road.

Taking the high road means making the healthiest decisions you can for your children no matter what you believe the other parent is doing. It means never lowering yourself to the other parent's level, putting the child in the middle, or making choices out of anger, frustration, resentment, or jealousy. This is particularly hard when the other parent is actively undermining the child's relationship with you.

Bobby comes home from Honey's house and tells his dad that he's a terrible father. Why doesn't he pay child support? Why did he leave Mom? To answer these questions is to put Bobby deeper in the middle of the adult conflict. The best possible way to answer is to help the child with his feelings without taking the bait. It may not be today or tomorrow, but Bobby will eventually recognize who his healthy parent is and will himself be healthier for the experience.

. . . .

CHAPTER SEVENTEEN

HIGHER AND HIRED POWERS

*One measure of maturity
is the realization that you
are capable of containing something
far bigger than yourself.*

Good health requires taking good care of yourself: exercising and eating a healthy diet, making careful choices, and relying on emotional anchors that refuel and support you. Our earliest emotional anchors, our parents, are chosen for us—for better or worse. But the autonomy that comes with letting go as we grow up and the process of constructing boundaries that define identity means the opportunity to choose new anchors.

Teenagers do this spontaneously, anchoring identity in the soccer team or a boy band or the martial arts; woodworking or NASCAR or math. These affiliations are often transitory, way stations that launch children toward adulthood, but sometimes not. Sometimes the groups and gangs and memberships that anchor us through adolescence become careers and avocations and the passions of adulthood.

Healthy adults do the same. We anchor larger or lesser bits of identity in clubs and charities and the arts, in our church or synagogue or mosque. We give and get support that refuels both self and community. We seek out these supports and we encourage our loved ones to do the same, confident in our maturity that the time and energies spent apart will refuel us and our children.

Pets

A dog or cat or any of a number of other common, domesticated species can become the embodiment of security. Perhaps more than others, these are animals that are cuddly, warm, and furry and that relish the opportunity to lick a hand and curl up in a bed. In this way they communicate holding, safety, and unadulterated love safety. Many people of many ages will confess that they tell all their secrets to their pets. Perhaps Fido's and Billy's heartbeat and breathing even falls into synchrony like mother and infant.

But more than providing security and comfort, a pet's birth or adoption and death are often a child's first experience of life cycle events. A chance to learn how to hold tight and then how to genuinely let go. That all relationships have a beginning, a middle, and an end. Letting go means grieving. Grief is painful, and it should be. It's a loss. Some parents want to rush right out and buy another puppy to bandage the wound, but as with any letting-go identity-building experience, managing the process is often the better choice. Showing the child that grief is survived, that Fido's memory goes on even after his body is done, is a lesson in holding tight and letting go unlike most others.

Psychotherapy

Psychotherapy can be a unique and valuable secondary anchor. If we define healthy adult relationships as reciprocal, and healthy parent-child relationships as a one-way street—parent giving to child—then good psychotherapy is more like the latter. A professional giving to a patient. Holding tight and letting go, over and over again. The therapist's constancy and the predictability of the routine serve to anchor and contain and help adjust the emotional thermostat. Psychotherapy can refuel and provide the means of carrying that precious emotional fuel around in a spare gas can, helping the patient improve his mpg.

The only expectation in return is payment.

Yes, you could sit alone in a room for an hour and say the same words out loud to no one for free, and this might actually help. We think about things differently when our words cycle out through the mouth and back in through the ears than when we just think the thoughts silently. Writing and reading in the form of journaling can work the same way. But even with the benefit of new perspective, psychotherapy is different. The relationship is the key.

The relatedness. The experiment of trusting. Of stepping back to understand how the lens of your personality might be distorting your perceptions. Of letting down the fortress-like boundaries or shoring up the sieve-like boundaries. Of discovering that your anger and sadness and fear can be expressed safely and maybe even can be let go.

There are dozens of different schools of psychotherapy: attitudes and beliefs and practices that shape how the therapist will approach you and define the relationship. There are also dozens of different degrees, certifications and licensures that qualify and legally enable a professional to provide the service. Understanding these details may be necessary, but is never sufficient for choosing a therapist. Your heart surgeon's credentials need to be stellar: The right schools. The right training and experience. The right word-of-mouth recommendations. But whether she understands your emotional needs or even speaks your language probably matters less or not at all.

Because psychotherapy is a relationship, it's ultimately more about the emotional fit between you and the professional than it is about the number of diplomas on the wall. It's about whether you feel comfortable and accepted, listened to and cared for. It's about the opportunity to feel emotionally held and how and when and why you're let go—one hour at a time over the course of weeks or months and sometimes years.

LETTING GO AND PSYCHOTHERAPY

Many contemporary psychotherapies offer practical fixes—specific tools that might help patients combat depression or anxiety, overcome specific phobias, or change certain behaviors. These have their place, but even these are most effective when the patient trusts the therapist and perceives him or her as skilled and caring.

Other types of psychotherapy (including the original Freudian psychoanalysis) rely largely on the quality of the therapist-patient relationship for change. Feeling held tight in therapy, struggling with being let go at the end of the therapy hour, and trusting that you will once again feel held tight at the same time next week (or sooner or later, depending on the therapy and the urgency of the situation) is critical to change. What happens in between and outside the therapy hour can therefore become at least as important—and often more so—than what happens in the therapy hour.

Letting go in therapy can be just as important as anything specifically discussed or planned or revealed in the therapy hour. The popular movies *What About Bob?* and *Anger Management* illustrate the idea humorously.

Religion

Religion anchors many in a way that pets, lovers, professionals, and even parents cannot. Trusting in a higher power; believing that your prayers are heard, even if they're not obviously answered; sharing these beliefs with others in worship; and accepting ideas like "God only gives us the burdens that we can bear" fuel confidence. That higher power—by any name, in any form—anchors its believers. Life and its trials are made understandable by casting them on a greater stage; defining them as the sequel to something that came before and the prelude to something that comes after: heaven or hell, the Elysian Fields or Valhalla, the gradual ascent to Nirvana, or a disintegration to return to the singularity. In the comfort of these immense and time-less and tireless arms, birth can be seen as letting go and death as a welcome return to being held tight.

Religious practices offer something more powerful even than religious beliefs—greater even than psychotherapy or your intimate partner or your mom or dad can offer. Religious practice is a constant that will never not be there. Your church or synagogue or mosque won't go away; even if the particular building somehow disappeared, there's always another. Spouses and therapists can die. They can get mad and reject us. They can move to a nicer climate. But lighting the candles on Friday night, saying Mass on Sunday morning, and unroll-ing the prayer rug five times each day are constants. Anchors.

Parents who endorse particular religious beliefs shore up their children's anchors by including them in the rituals. Teaching them to wear the clothes, to observe the routines, and to adopt the beliefs can instill a sense of security that is far greater than what Mom or Dad can offer on their own. Religious affiliation, belief, and practice can shape identity and personality for a lifetime.

But religion is not unique in providing these anchors. College alumni associations, sororities and fraternities, ethnic organizations, and twelve step programs for addictions each offer some of the same. The ritual is constant. The practices are unchanging. If you're on busi-ness in Miami or Mozambique, vacationing in Sante Fe or Sarajevo, you know that you are connected and you belong.

Practical Pointer:

SOPHIE'S CHOICE

Just as the Meryl Streep character in the well-known movie faced an impossible choice, we are sometimes forced to choose between unhealthy and conflicting anchors. The chameleon child may be forced to choose between his warring parents. The adulti-fied or parentified child must choose between a needy parent and a peer group. Belonging to one club or group or religion may require renouncing another.

Under certain circumstances, a choice of this nature may make sense. Most employers reasonably insist that you not also work for the competition. Most psychotherapists will at least request that if you're in another, simultaneous therapy, that the professionals involved be allowed to coordinate their efforts. But if a friend or lover or group or religion insists that you cut ties with another anchor in order to be accepted, this may not be healthy. Any relationship genuinely interested in your well-being will encourage you to enjoy as many healthy supports as you can find.

· · · · · · · · · ·

CHAPTER EIGHTEEN

THE EMPTY NEST

*Finishing is both
the best and the worst
part of any task.*

I'm a fan of the space program. I've watched *Apollo* and space shuttle launches in person and on TV with little-boy, Freudian awe over the incredible size and power of the vehicles. Man-made volcanic eruptions pushing thousands of tons of hardware up through the atmosphere. Blue skies turn to black void where, with nanosecond precision, the vast bulk of the vehicle is jettisoned, freeing a pod the size of a school bus to fly into the infinity of space.

This is letting go on a grand scale. A handful of astronauts contained in a high-tech tin can moving many times the speed of sound, hoping and trusting that their million mile anchor rope is secure; that they will return healthy and whole someday to once again be held tight by gravity.

As parents, we take off the training wheels and run alongside our children, holding tight and letting go. We drop them at day care, at preschool, at their first day of kindergarten and then high school and college, holding tight and letting go. We launch them like astronauts, off on a long explore, holding tight and letting go. In their eyes we are Mother Earth, their anchor, constant and confident, ready to embrace them upon their return.

But there we stand, panting from the exertion and watching them ride off down the sidewalk. Now we're suddenly alone at the bus stop or in the car, the warmth of his body slowly dissipating from the fabric of his booster seat. We're alone back at home after the U-Haul has been returned, after the wet towels that you begged him to launder are finally picked up off the floor, after the sheets have been changed and his bed has been made, ready for his return.

Now what?

The parent's experience of being left behind can be like that of the towering cylindrical fuel cells that the astronauts eject once they are spent, obsolete and empty; baggage allowed to slowly degrade in the fiery atmosphere. It can be like Shel Silverstein's *Giving Tree*, content to be emptied and mutilated, amputated and forgotten. But it doesn't have to be that way.

Although our young children must not be our emotional anchors, they do fill our lives. It's easy to spend two decades or more—a full quarter of many people's life spans—consumed with changing diapers and packing lunches and checking homework; with chauffeuring to and from schools and appointments and practices and games and recitals and friends' houses, in total a distance undoubtedly farther even than astronauts might travel. And then with a little luck and a lot of practice, they leave.

It's easy, too, to anticipate that letting go will be freeing. Reason for a party. A chance to get your old life back, no matter that the life you're referring to is now only vaguely remembered, was never as good as you think it was, and fits who you are today about as well as the clothes you wore at the time. Okay, so go ahead and throw an "empty nest" party.

Now what?

Now the adultifying and parentifying and infantilizing parent goes into crisis. The pathology of role reversal means that this parent can only let go when the adult's distorted need is filled by another enabling victim, and then the parent-child separation is abrupt and complete. But when the parent lacks a replacement, the child remains the adult's anchor, and the anchor must never be too far away. This parent has a convenient medical crisis, an accidental overdose, a car accident—"but it wasn't my fault!"—or a fall into the depths of depression that requires the newly launched child to rush home to the parent's rescue. Mission aborted. Even the monstrous engines of the space shuttle couldn't escape this parent's gravity.

The parent of the chameleon child, the polarized child, and the alienated child retreats behind his fortress-like and impenetrable boundaries, intolerant of any dissenting beliefs. Surrounded by similarly closed-minded sycophants. She may welcome her son home in the same way that she offered security all along—conditionally; my way or the highway—only to discover that, once launched, the boy begins to shed the empty and artificial identity that was foist upon him. Long overdue conflict erupts. The anchor rope becomes frayed and then breaks even as the child and his other, healthier parent, begin to reconnect.

But for healthy parents like you and me—having given of ourselves freely, having launched our children eagerly, and always being willing to anchor them unconditionally—the empty nest means an opportunity to rediscover self. To redefine identity and personality and relationships. To rebalance the ratio of emotional giving and getting. And to approach these adventures with renewed energy, far greater maturity, and the wisdom of one who is fulfilled by having given so much.

Who Are Your Anchors?

Start by renewing your experience of feeling held tight. This might be as sensual or sexual as it sounds, but it might be as mundane as simply paying your dues. Rejoining the club. Planning a Thursday night book group and setting aside every other Saturday as "date night." These are structures—limits and boundaries and routines—that reduce anxiety and refuel confidence, freeing you to let go, secure in the knowledge of what awaits you upon your return.

Remember how Bouncing Baby Billy used to toddle over, arms uplifted, asking to be held? You were there to pick him up and hold him tight without reservation. You refueled him gladly and unconditionally, and then sent him back out to explore again. You've done this a million times and you'll gladly do it a million times more, as long as you are able.

But when you toddle over to your intimate partner asking to be held tight, it's different. The relationship is a two-way street, so holding tight and letting go is about both giving and getting. Somehow you worked out terms that lasted through the kids' childhoods, but the kids are gone now, so it's time to renegotiate. You can't ask how you're going to get held without also asking what your partner needs. The outcome will seldom be exactly reciprocal, but it needs to feel constant and sufficient to each of you. It needs to feel like an anchor.

That's just one anchor. Maybe it's even your biggest anchor. But you'll need more.

Indeed, a healthy adult relationship may be necessary, but it can never be sufficient. As adults, we needs lots of anchors to hold us tight, the same way that we need lots of different foods to fuel our bodies. We need relationships that make us laugh and make us think. We need relationships that challenge us to grow and reflect, and relationships that give us escape; that make us feel good in body and mind.

Who these people or groups or activities are and how these needs are met must be part of the negotiation. Getting there requires that partners share confidence and trust and communication. We must not only have a mutual willingness to put the cards on the table, so we can say "hold me tight" and "let me go," but we must also have the freedom and independence to say, "Don't go" and "Please, give me some space."

Apex and Apogee

Launching our children off, into the void, is letting go as much for us as it is for them. Parent and child are each freed from many of the limits and boundaries and routines that have held them for years—for the child's entire life—and are therefore free to create identity, personality, and relationships anew.

There is a unique kind of parallel process in this moment. It is a developmental epoch during which parent and child are briefly working on the same tasks of growing up. The empty nest parent and the newly launched child are simultaneously but separately testing the limits of their new freedoms, redrawing the boundaries of identity, and exploring long-awaited opportunities. The parallel can be as obvious and awkward and sitcom-like as the single mom and young adult daughter who are both dating, or the father who goes back to school and finds himself in his college-aged son's classes. But the moment is usually as subtle as it is critical. Either way, it marks a shift in the quality of the parent-child relationship.

It is only now, in this moment of developmental synchrony, that parent and child each have the emotional maturity to see one another as real human beings. To allow one another to have genuine needs and wishes, fears and desires. While the parent remains the child's emotional anchor, the child—like the parent—has many other anchors as well. These may include similar-aged friends, groups and clubs, and perhaps even intimate partners. This removes some of the pressure from the emotional umbilicus that connects parent and child, allowing them to orient to other anchors while relating to one another.

Roles change in this moment. It's not that parent and child become peers—Mom and Dad are still anchors in the child's life—but they might become co-adults. They recognize that they face similar challenges and can learn from each other. Even help one another. They both pay bills and they both argue with bosses; they both get constipated and they both have dreams and goals and fears.

The stereotype has fathers and sons bonding over beers, hunting or fishing or building something in the garage or the backyard together. Mothers and daughters shop or bake or cook or share social and cultural events. The setting, the activity, and the excuse hardly matter. Respect grows in these shared moments, sometimes in laughter, sometimes in anger, sometimes in tears, and a new kind of communication appears. The calls from college home become less one sided—parent giving and child getting—and more mutual. This often starts with THS: Technology Helplessness Syndrome.

Our children are native-born speakers of a technology that we learn as a second language, if at all. Today that means all things digital, but the phenomenon is universal. Once upon a time, cave-mom had to ask cave-son which plants to grind up to make the really cool reddish color he used to draw the bison on the cave wall. There was a time when father asked son how to start the Model-T, how to get Marge (the proverbial party-line operator) on the line, how to dial (and I really mean dial) the telephone, how to tune the radio or fix the arm on the phonograph or run the eight-track player or untangle the cassette tape.

Just a year or two ago, the problem was programming the VCR. Remember VCRs? Today we worry about the GPS that directs you to a restaurant in Istanbul and whether the router and the modem are compatible and why the video won't stream. Passwords are forgotten and accounts are hacked and, while we're on the subject, what is the cloud, anyway?

So we begin reaching out to our children for help with these new obstacles. After all, they eat and breathe this stuff. Our weakness is their opportunity to shine. They do so with more or less patience, more or less condescending ridicule, and more or less skill, but when they do this, they become our anchors in a very small way. Your next call to your son or daughter about a restaurant in Istanbul will start to sound more and more like Bouncing Baby Billy's whine from across the room and accomplish the same thing. Both are requests to be held tight.

The rocket that our kids are riding is on its way up and away. The rocket that we've been riding is on its way down. Here we pass, ships in the night, the seesaw balance between holding tight and letting go resting at equilibrium for a fleeting moment, and then the moment passes. It might be tomorrow or forty years from now but inevitably, inexorably, the roles will reverse. Age and illness and infirmity catch up with us all.

Practical Pointer:

HOLDING TIGHT BY PROXY

Our children grow back and forth, gradually moving farther and farther away from their anchors. They carry transitional objects and develop transitional affiliations; perhaps they even find intimate partners to anchor them next door or half a planet away. As healthy parents, we do what we can to ensure that their needs are met, but we're left on our own to manage our needs without them.

This is as it should be, but the dilemma is real. Some empty-nest parents turn to hobbies and work and re-establish their intimate relationships. And some feel the need with or without these steps to hold tight to others. These are adults who find caregiving fulfilling, who accept that it's time to let their own kids go, and who look for surrogates or proxies to hold tight instead.

For some of these parents, it's not an empty nest so much as a furry nest. Cats and dogs remain our babies and companions long after the kids grow up and move out. Holding tight and letting go of a pet is more a matter of how far you let out the leash, confident that Fido or Fluffy will always come home at night.

Others take in foster children, volunteer as CASA (Court Appointed Special Advocate) workers in the courts, or participate in youth support programs through a church, synagogue, mosque, or community. Unfortunately, there is never not a need for healthy, able, and willing caregivers in any number of similar capacities.

· · · · · · · · · ·

CHAPTER NINETEEN

FULL CIRCLE

The best gift
is to give what is genuinely needed.
The second best gift
is to receive the same in return.

Like every good story, this one ends back where it began. At the beginning. We have two people bound by an emotional bond, one the anchor and the other anchored. One establishes structure so that the other can feel contained. One holds tight so that the other can let go.

The difference now is that the roles have reversed. Parent is reduced to childlike needs and child is forced to carry parent-like burdens. Sometimes this happens abruptly: A blood vessel erupts in the brain. A clot blocks the flow of blood. A heart skips a beat. And sometimes it happens gradually: Plaque accumulates. Vessels clog. Dopamine is depleted. A lump metastasizes. The lungs turn grayer and grayer and then black. Whether the change is sudden or slow, in the end we are more like cars than the mpg metaphor suggests. Our parts break and our engines fail sooner or—with the right genes, careful maintenance, and good luck—sometimes later.

When a parent dies suddenly, her children are left in shock to try to understand the empty place at the dinner table. They are cast adrift, anchored by her memory, the transitional objects that still carry her scent and sound and image, and the groups that share some small measure of the loss. Grief is the excruciating process of editing the absent parent out of each of a million tiny expectations while simultaneously fighting to recapture the past.

When a parent dies slowly, failing bit by bit in mind or body or both, the shock is delayed and dulled; it's ushered in by denial. His doctor ordered blood tests? That's routine. He's in chemo? Just a precaution. The doctor said it's fifty-fifty? Don't worry, he'll beat the odds. He'll be fine. He always lands on his feet.

Until he doesn't. Until his strength ebbs, the pain takes over, and the body's thermostat fails, throwing appetite and sleep and toileting and moods and memory all out of whack. Although medicine, specialists, and procedures might help, the advocacy needed to get them, and the organization needed to keep track of them, require a staff of full-time administrators with advanced degrees in nursing, accounting, and biochemistry.

It is far more than ironic—it is simply criminal—that the people with the fewest resources in our society receive the least support.

Doctors don't talk to each other. Insurance companies argue about covering promised or promising procedures, as if time didn't matter, while the fuse on the time-bomb burns away; while every breath hurts. The pills prescribed could fill buckets and then bathtubs and then swimming pools until you could dive in headfirst and never be seen again. Medicines potentiate one another, create side effects and allergic reactions and addictions that are worse than the problems they were prescribed to resolve.

But most harmful of all is the pummeling, unrelenting assault on dignity. This is the anonymous, assembly-line, take-a-number, take-off-your-clothes, say-ahh, spread-em-wide erosion of self that most patients must eventually endure. I understand it—medical professionals are vulnerable to burn out their compassion muscles more easily than weight lifters blow out their biceps—but I can't excuse it. Nor should you.

And so, brought to our knees by pain, ignorance, and fear; insulted by the impossible costs of uncertain cures; and insulted yet again by the degrading humiliation of it all, we are all ultimately re-duced to a childlike neediness. We are left praying that someone will hold the handlebars and run alongside, not to launch us on our way, but to hold us tight until the training wheels can be refastened. We need someone to make sense out of the chaos. To impose structure. To sort the buckets of pills into morning and midday and supper-time doses. To label the cabinets and to hide the knives. To clean up the bathroom or the bedsheets or our diapers. To come when we call—when anxiety tips the seesaw balance away from independence—to hold us tight and then, when the time is right, to let us go.

Child as Anchor

The parentified or adultified child only pretends to be her mother's emotional anchor. She might revel in the specialness of her prema-ture promotion into adulthood, but her separateness is an illusion. Cheated out of childhood, the child is enmeshed with her parent. Oceanic. Without the opportunity and experience of genuinely let-ting go, discovering self, she is no more her mother's emotional anchor than the parent's own shadow. A reflection in the narcissist's mirror.

With the benefit of time and healthy parenting, a child has a chance to build a coherent identity. He becomes a drip fully emerged from the ocean; he learns how to regulate his own body and emotions. Armed with hard-won confidence (and a teddy bear or his teammates or his girlfriend, as the situation demands), he can go out in the world and test new anchors. The team drops him? The girlfriend breaks up with him? He comes home to be refueled and then he's off again, wiser for the experience and more likely to succeed.

These are the experiences that build the emotional strength a growing child needs to someday anchor someone else. To explore a mature, reciprocal relationship with an intimate partner. To relish the miraculous and exhausting process of raising a child. And maybe even to care for an ailing and aging parent.

In some cultures and at some points in history, the aged and in-firm were venerated; revered; respected for the wisdom accumulated over the course of a lifetime and through the trial of their pain. In these cultures, children grew up expecting to care for their parents in their later years. The experience was an honor and a privilege, bringing parent and child full circle.

It is embarrassing to admit that we live in a culture and a time that ignores and neglects the elderly and infirm. Their wisdom is often dismissed as irrelevant. Their memories are forgotten. Their pain is relegated to back wards and cubbyhole rooms shared with strangers. The cruelty and stupidity of this process is only exceeded by its shortsightedness. We conveniently forget that we will all someday be old and ill. We will all someday need, once again, to be held tight. It's hard to imagine that a financial nest egg of any size, a long-term care insurance policy of any value, or a nursing home of any quality could ever replace the loving embrace of our own children.

The psychology of the matter is simple: Having come full circle, the healthy adult child anchors and refuels her dying parent, holding tight and then, finally, generously, letting go. The process is a gift to all involved far greater than its costs. It's a comfort to one unparalleled by any medication or nurse or hospital, and it conveys to the other a confidence and maturity and perspective that can be earned in no other way. Having cared for her parent in death, the adult child may be grief-stricken, but is also made whole, better able to care for herself and for her children; secure in the idea that they will someday be there for her, to hold her tight and to let her go.

Of course, the reality of the matter is far more complex. We live in a fast-paced, me-here-now society. The bills must be paid. The wheels must keep turning at all costs. Humanity and emotions and relationships are often relegated to the back burner, trumped by the demands made by the boss and the landlord and the bill collector. We rationalize that our absence from our parents' lives in their declining years is the norm, that they insist that we live our lives, and that our own children need us now. These statements may be true, but they're not enough. The whole of identity over the course of a lifetime requires not only that we are held tight and let go, but also that we learn how to hold others tight and then let them go.

Practical Pointer:

DEATH, RELIGION, AND LETTING GO

Helping your children understand and cope with death can be essential to their understanding of letting go. Religion often sets the stage for this process.

Religions that teach that there is an afterlife can both comfort and confuse children. On the one hand, the idea that Grandpa is in heaven sidesteps unanswerable questions about mortality and the finite. On the other hand, the idea that "Grandpa is looking down on you" has prompted many children to feel that all privacy has been lost.

No matter your religious beliefs, practices, or affiliations, the message we must give our children is that all living things have a beginning, a middle, and an end. We are held tight at the beginning and the end, and we are let go in between.

CHAPTER TWENTY

· · · · · · · · · ·

ONE

Who am I
if we're never apart?

A critical assumption underlies this book and my thinking and, I would venture, rests somewhere deep inside your head too. The fact that we may share this assumption doesn't make it correct. Leaving it unspoken only compounds my error and cheats you, dear reader, of the opportunity to better understand yourself and your children.

At one point, thanks to the fluidity of writing in a digital medium, I actually went back and inserted a new first chapter explaining my assumption in the belief that it colors all that follows. It does, but I soon realized that asking you to wrestle with this assumption from the start distracted from the next chapter and the chapter after that. As a result, I really do end here where I once began, offering as coda a preface relevant to all that you just read.

Holding tight and letting go are about the development of identity. Defining self. The individual. I've hinted here and there about how two individuals can share an identity at birth, how love and physical intimacies can erode the boundaries that differentiate people at least briefly, and how pathologically enmeshed relationships can compromise development. But through it all, I've generally assumed that the healthy and mature individual constitutes one whole and complete identity.

Ants and bees and *Star Trek's* alien race called the Borg and the cells in your body and the stars in the sky, given a voice, would all disagree. Each is part of a larger whole. The insects and the Borg are part of a colony or hive just as your cells are parts of organs or limbs which, in turn, are parts of your body. The stars are parts of galaxies and constellations and the universe.

You are and should be respected as a complete individual unto yourself, but you reached this state gradually, as a result of cells dividing and differentiating, systems holding tight and letting go, and those systems themselves being held tight and then let go within larger systems. Self within family, family within neighborhood, neighborhood within community. Your identity is a cookie-cutter shape cut from the doughy fabric of the relationships within your family, and your family itself has its own identity cut cookie-cutter-like from the fabric of the community, which itself . . . well, you get it.

It all sounds very Escher-like—a disorienting din that threatens disintegration; loss of self within a fractal chain of nested wholes. The fact is, nonetheless, that how we define *ONE* turns out to be a matter of perspective. A statistical comparison of variance within and variance between. The difference between looking through a microscope and looking through a telescope. For example, it's easy to say that you now hold a book, but is this book just one component part of a library the way that your leg is one component part of you? Is it a couple hundred individual pages? Is it thousands of words, or hundreds of thousands of printed alphanumeric symbols, or millions of pixels?

The Internet and terrorism and disease and global warming, among many other contemporary geopolitical and psychological pressures, are forcing us to reconsider how we define *ONE*. Our ideas of separateness, relatedness, and identity are shifting.

On one hand, the boundaries that distinguish my thoughts and feelings and sensations from yours are quickly dissolving. We are now more interconnected and hive-like as a species than in all of history. Groupthink is real. Crowdsourcing happens. The images that we see and the sounds that we hear (although so far not the smells, tastes, or textures that we experience) can be instantly and constantly

and universally shared. But more than a matter of choice and pa-
rental controls, closed-circuit TV and search engine trackers, phone
record leaks and GPS signals, RFID technologies, vendors who sell
our spending preferences to ad agencies, the Patriot Act and Edward
Snowden's revelations blur the distinction between my internal experience and yours. The separateness of my thoughts and feelings is
quickly eroding, a drip falling back into the ocean from whence it
first came. Privacy is going the way of the mastodon, no matter what
HIPAA promises.

On the other hand, the boundaries that separate our bodies are
being fortified. The physical distance between you and me is increasing. The proof is in the Purell.[5]

Purell is one of several popular hand-sanitizing gels that are now
available universally. Chances are that there is a dispenser of the slimy
and satisfying goop somewhere near you right now. The sales of these
products have skyrocketed in recent years, but no one knows whether
this is the result of an epidemic of germophobia, or its cause. No
matter, the effect is the same: Anxiety about physical contact now
runs rampant in our society. Hypervigilance about germs and viruses
and microbes, contamination and illness and mortality—this is all
the new normal. We keep our distance and reinforce the bubbles that
define personal space today because we fear vectors, not violence. We
see one another as carriers of disease.

Those who washed their hands ten or twelve or twenty times
each day in the 1990s were either conscientious health care workers
or people who had obsessive compulsive disorder. Today, it's expected.
You'll seldom find a continuous cloth towel dispenser next to the sink
in a public restroom. Even traditional paper towel dispensers are being
replaced in favor of automatic motion-detecting, no-touch machines
and blow driers. Toilet flushers and doorknobs and light switches are
looked upon in fear and creatively manipulated to avoid touch when

---

5. As much as I've resisted the urge to pepper this text with citations, David Owen's
March 4, 2013, article, "Hands Across America" in the *New Yorker* is well worth your
time. Find it online at http://www.newyorker.com/magazine/2013/03/04/hands-
across-america.

no one's looking. We sneeze into our elbows. Fist bumps replace hand-shakes. Airplane passengers wear respiratory masks formerly seen only in operating rooms. And these are just the publicly visible symptoms.

What no one can see is how many people are staying home. How many potential cruise line passengers never bought tickets because stomach viruses are part of many ships' all-inclusive fare? How many office workers and executives Skype or FaceTime or use GoToMeeting online, not because travel is expensive and time consuming, but because going out means exposure? Meeting face-to-face is as yesterday as the typewriter.

These simultaneous and divergent trends—the breakdown of the boundaries between internal selves and the fortification of the boundaries between external selves—are both increasing exponentially. Each feeds on itself. Online activity breeds more online activity and can become an addiction to the point that many relationships exist today nowhere but on Facebook. Log on to hold tight. Reboot to let go.

Isolation breeds more isolation. Never tested, a fear can never be disproven. Worse, by avoiding germs, our immune systems are weakened, making the fear that first motivated avoidance more and more real.

I wouldn't bother you with this existential and philosophical rant if it had nothing to do with parenting. It does. In fact, it cuts to the quick of who we are, how we raise our children, how and when and where and why we let go and hold tight.

Every parent faces the dilemma inherent in instilling the last generation's values, beliefs and practices in their children, just as every child faces the dilemma of rejecting Mom's and Dad's old-fashioned ways. This is part of letting go. It's part of the angst that must erupt in adolescence and why transitional affiliations—groups and clubs and cliques and gangs—are so important. The fight often comes up about clothing, in particular. Mom thinks that Honey's skirt is too short. Her friends think that it's the cat's meow.

But what happens if the difference from one generation to the next raises questions about the basic nature of identity and relatedness? These are questions that every child through all of time has had to manage, but always before with the benefit of their parents' advice and example. I fear that that no longer applies.

The evidence is all around us. I've seen parents text their children across the dinner table to ask for the ketchup. I know children who have never played sports or been on a team, but who lead a hoard of warriors in pursuit of treasure for hours every day. And I know many, many families that argue constantly about screen time—how long a child should be in front of his computer, laptop, or tablet or on his phone Tweeting and Instagramming and Pinteresting and iTuning and YouTubing. The parents want the kids to go out and play. Swing on a swing. Slide on a slide. Get dirty. Throw a ball. Build a snowman. They argue that sun and sweat and physical activity are important. Me? I think they're right. But we share a generation and, to a greater or lesser degree, we share an affliction.

Technology Helplessness Syndrome.

The children argue that outside is dangerous and lonely. The playground is empty. All of their friends are online. The child whom we once thought of as the geek or the nerd and worried that he would miss out is now a Minecraft Master, hosting hundreds of "friends" in his domain.

See? That's the problem. I put *friends* in quotes as if they're not real. If I were Tweeting right now, you'd hear the argument in my head: They're not real! They'll never meet. They'll never exchange birthday presents or . . . what? Cheat off one another's tests in math class? Friends do that. And these kids might too. More and more education is being conducted online. Brains converge while bodies remain distant. Students cheat via Xbox and text message while they do square roots on their laptops, peering over one another's virtual shoulders, even though they're miles apart.

Play together? But isn't that what they're doing? They play dress-up and pretend without all the bother of scissors and glue and scraps of construction paper scattered across the kitchen floor. They play tag, even though it's with light sabers and without burning calories. If they want to play football, they can join teams scattered around the planet playing Madden NFL. If they want to drive a car or fly a plane or slay a dragon, they can do all of this too. And they don't have to ever be alone.

But at what cost? Aside from the dollars, the cost of sitting in front of a screen rather than running across a field is atrophy, obesity, and a failure to develop gross motor skills even as hand-eye and fine motor skills are being honed to a mouse-clicking, joy-sticking razor's edge. If culture continues to evolve in its present direction, maybe the child forced to go out and get dirty will be at a disadvantage in tomorrow's world. Maybe spending five hours every day (and ten on weekends) in front of a screen for ten or twelve years will be prerequisite to tomorrow's jobs.

And maybe in pursuit of those jobs, our children won't even need to write a résumé. Why would they? Everything an employer might need to know is right there, online: every keystroke and Google search and Amazon purchase and peek at pornography they've made; every grade earned and bill paid; and every text and Tweet and post and blog they have ever written. It's not too sci-fi to even imagine that our kids won't be hired individually, because the individual will have been subsumed within a task-oriented undifferentiated ego mass. Not a team or a group in the antiquated sense, but a superordinate self-cluster with a single shared identity and a proven track record racing cars or killing dragons or building cubical worlds. Why would an employer hire an individual if he can hire a hive?

And so we must reframe holding tight and letting go within the emerging digital era. We must try to shake off the preconceptions we bring forward from our days as analogue children, each separate from the other, and try to understand how boundaries and identity and relationships exist today and try to prepare for a brand-new tomorrow.

I can see it now: There will be no more physical letting go. The world will be much too scary to allow a child to toddle off away from Mom or to ride a two-wheeler, even though the bicycles that still exist will be gyroscopically self-correcting, GPS tracked, and air bag–enabled. No more training wheels. Billy will have a motion-activated virtual reality surround where we used to hang the black-and-white mobile above the crib. When his anxiety escalates, heart rate and respiratory monitors will cue an immediate, full-sensory virtual-mom reality right there and then, as instant and almost as fulfilling as what the fetus experienced in the womb. As heart rate and respirations slow, the full-sensory mom experience will transition effortlessly to an experience of shared warm and gentle and psychologically engineered sounds, shapes, and movements. Other infants will be present in every way except physically from their surrounds in their own cribs far away. There is no risk of contracting any disease or sustaining any injury during this playdate. Together, this ever-shifting, multinational, geographically and ethnically and religiously unbounded group will coo and gaa-gaa and drool and develop a mutual sense of self. A group-me. Identities will be built during this let-go until, fatigued or overwhelmed, hungry or tired, the child will set off sensors that will communicate physiological cues, the playgroup will fade away, and Mom will come back into focus to hold tight, pixilated in high definition complete with digitally enhanced, genetically tailored scents and smells and nurturance.

Is this a future to be feared or welcomed or simply expected in the due course of evolution? I've been startled by the number of people who read this final chapter as a dire prediction, as if the evolution of self is a kind of Armageddon. I really struggle to understand this perspective, particularly in light of the fact that none of these people are Luddites. Each Tweets and texts and otherwise submerges themselves in the digital continuum, surrendering privacy and autonomy one megabyte at a time.

It's not that I am eager for this outcome. I like being me, separate and unique from you, at least as much as you likely feel the same in return. But if we step back far enough to try to see around our cultural blind spots and our ego defenses, the trend is clear. Our children and their children and their children after them will be more and more physically separate even as they become less and less emotionally and cognitively and sensually independent. Perhaps this agglomeration is similar to what early hominids encountered as cave dwellers came together to share the hunt, or what early settlers encountered as towns coalesced in the old west. Maybe this is what families experienced as the Industrial Revolution brought workers into tight quarters, housing many families in a single building, or what college students experience today as they move into rabbit-warren-like dormitories. In each of these and in hundreds of other similar examples, separateness was traded in for mutual benefit. Privacy and autonomy were reduced in the interest of survival.

Even if you dismiss this idea as so much sci-fi nonsense, one observation remains simple and clear and relevant to the parenting decisions that you make every day. You can only hold your children tight so long. When you finally take off the training wheels and let them go, they ride away not only across the visible space in front of you, but also out into an infinitely vast ocean of words and images and ideas and experiences that threatens—for better or worse—to draw them in. You can insist that they wear a bike helmet. You can install virus protection, pop-up blockers, spam catchers, and keystroke trackers, but you can protect their identities no more than you can protect their knees. They must fall down... and they'll need you there, once again, to hold them tight.

From vast and boundless ocean
to contained and confident drip
and back again.
This is the evolution of the self,
the evolution of the species
and the evolution of the universe.

INDEX OF TOPICS

About Dr. Garber

Ben Garber is a New Hampshire licensed psychologist with a special interest in serving the
needs of children. His interest working as an
individual and family therapist, Guardian ad
litem, parenting coordinator and consultant
to the courts is in better understanding and
serving the needs of children.

Dr. Garber is a renowned speaker and a
prolific, award-winning author. He has had
the privilege of addressing audiences across the United States and
Canada. His "Healthy Parent" column has appeared in popular press
publications across the English-speaking world for more than fifteen
years. His numerous peer-reviewed professional publications and
eight books have helped to assure that families and family law process
are child-centered.

Dr. Garber is a proud son and husband. He is the father of two
adult children. He resides in New Hampshire and can often be found
kayaking and fishing on the remote lakes of northern New England.

Learn more about holding tight and letting go, about Dr. Garber
and his practice at www.HealthyParent.com.

CPSIA information can be obtained at www.ICGtesting.com
Printed in the USA
LVOW10s0311180216

475486LV00007B/26/P